Cedar Breaks National Monument
Geologic Resource Evaluation Report

Natural Resource Report NPS/NRPC/GRD/NRR—2006/006

Geologic Resources Division
Natural Resource Program Center
P.O. Box 25287
Denver, Colorado 80225

March 2006

U.S. Department of the Interior
Washington, D.C.

The Natural Resource Publication series addresses natural resource topics that are of interest and applicability to a broad readership in the National Park Service and to others in the management of natural resources, including the scientific community, the public, and the NPS conservation and environmental constituencies. Manuscripts are peer-reviewed to ensure that the information is scientifically credible, technically accurate, appropriately written for the intended audience, and is designed and published in a professional manner.

Natural Resource Reports are the designated medium for disseminating high priority, current natural resource management information with managerial application. The series targets a general, diverse audience, and may contain NPS policy considerations or address sensitive issues of management applicability. Examples of the diverse array of reports published in this series include vital signs monitoring plans; "how to" resource management papers; proceedings of resource management workshops or conferences; annual reports of resource programs or divisions of the Natural Resource Program Center; resource action plans; fact sheets; and regularly-published newsletters.

Views and conclusions in this report are those of the authors and do not necessarily reflect policies of the National Park Service. Mention of trade names or commercial products does not constitute endorsement or recommendation for use by the National Park Service.

Printed copies of reports in these series may be produced in a limited quantity and they are only available as long as the supply lasts. This report is also available from the Geologic Resource Evaluation Program website (http://www2.nature.nps.gov/geology/inventory/gre_publications) on the internet, or by sending a request to the address on the back cover. Please cite this publication as:

Thornberry-Ehrlich, T. 2006. Cedar Breaks National Monument Geologic Resource Evaluation Report. Natural Resource Report NPS/NRPC/GRD/NRR—2006/006. National Park Service, Denver, Colorado.

NPS D-215, March 2006

Table of Contents

List of Figures

Executive Summary

This report has been developed to accompany the digital geologic map produced by Geologic Resource Evaluation staff for Cedar Breaks National Monument. It contains information relevant to resource management and scientific research.

Cedar Breaks National Monument provides visitors the rare opportunity of standing in one physiographic province while viewing a panorama of an entirely different physiographic province. Visitors standing on the nearly flat- lying strata of the Colorado Plateau can look to the west at the stark landscape of the Basin and Range province.

This splendid view is eclipsed only by the multicolored cliffs, spires, pinnacles, and other geologic features carved by erosion and weathering into the natural amphitheaters just below the rim, or "break" in the gently east- dipping, pine- covered surface of the plateau. The geologic processes of weathering and erosion are vividly captured in stone and yet, are not static. Relentlessly working towards a dynamic equilibrium, these processes shape and reshape the landscape treating visitors to a changing and vibrant viewscape.

The Markagunt Plateau is a small part of the High Plateaus region of the Colorado Plateau Physiographic province. Cedar Breaks forms the western escarpment of the Markagunt Plateau delineating the boundary between the Colorado Plateau and the Basin and Range Physiographic Provinces. The unparalleled geologic variety of the region attracted over 514,000 visitors in 2004. Visitors are drawn by the myriad of rock shapes including columns, spires, hoodoos, windows, pedestals, bridges, alcoves, and canyons, and other spectacular geological features carved into the red, orange, and white fluvial and lacustrine strata of the Claron Formation. Although visitors appreciate the geologic wonders of Cedar Breaks their very numbers place increasing demands on available resources.

Understanding the geology of Cedar Breaks enhances one's understanding of the unique relationship between geology and the environment. Geology provides the foundation of the entire ecosystem. In Cedar Breaks National Monument surface exposures consist primarily of Cretaceous, Tertiary, and Quaternary age rocks. Rock layers are exposed by erosion of the Markagunt Plateau, revealing clues about the varied environments responsible for creating the present landscape. Knowing the geology in detail is fundamental to determining the history of Cedar Breaks National Monument and to managing and preserving geologic features today.

Geologic processes initiate complex responses that give rise to rock formations, surface and subsurface fluid movement, soils, and canyons. Preservation of the canyons, spires, alcoves, and hoodoos of Cedar Breaks National Monument is absolutely necessary for the continued inspiration of wonder in park visitors.

Emphasis of geologic resources both in natural resource management and in educational program is certain to enhance the visitor's experience.

Cedar Breaks National Monument, which mirrors the multi- colored landscape of Bryce Canyon National Park, its better known neighbor 40 miles to the east, hosts some of the most spectacular desert erosional features on earth. The interplay of geology, water, tectonic forces, and climate created this architectural elegance on the landscape at Cedar Breaks. Some of the principal geologic issues and concerns for the monument pertain to protecting these features. Humans have modified the landscape surrounding Cedar Breaks and consequently have altered the natural geologic processes. These processes are dynamic and capable of noticeably changing the landscape within a human life span (less than a century). The following features, issues, and processes have been identified as having the most geological importance and the highest level of management significance to the monument:

- Slope failures and slope processes. Arid, desert environments are especially susceptible to slumping and landslide problems due to the lack of stabilizing plant growth and the relatively frequent occurrence of intense seasonal rainstorms. Construction of roads and trails also impacts the stability of a slope. Mudstone-rich units such as the Brian Head Formation are typically found in outcrop as slopes. These slopes are prone to fail when saturated. In addition the more resistant units in the monument are exposed as cliffs and precipitous slopes. Rockfall and slope failure is a potential hazard almost everywhere along the roads and trails of Cedar Breaks National Monument.

- Seismic and mining activity. Cedar Breaks was created to preserve and protect some of the most spectacular erosional spires and other geologic features in the world, yet this area is still seismically active. In addition to natural seismicity, vibrations from blasting at nearby mines are also putting these features at risk.

- Fracturing and karst development in the Claron Formation. The Tertiary age Claron Formation forms the spectacular hoodoos and other erosional features that delight visitors. However, the fractures and sinkholes inherent in the formation also pose serious threats to overlooks and other visitor facilities. Caves may also play a cultural resource role at the monument.

- Water Issues. The southern Utah mountains receive on average about 8- 10 inches of precipitation each year with higher altitudes receiving more. This sparse rainfall defines the arid climate that makes water such an important resource regionally. Water for Cedar Breaks National Monument comes primarily from wells drawing water from aquifers in the Claron Formation and Straight Cliffs Sandstone. Productive aquifers must be deep enough to be relatively impervious to drought conditions and be contained in fractured rock that provides groundwater conduits to the well. The hydrogeologic system at the monument is not well understood and warrants further study.

Other geologic issues such as the paleontological potential of the area, wind erosion, hoodoo formation and preservation, faulting and deformation processes, and the story of the Marysvale Volcanic Field, were also identified as important management issues for Cedar Breaks National Monument.

It is the interaction of the variety of rock types with the topographic landscape created by uplift and erosion that must be understood to assess potential hazards and best protect the visitors to the park. The Map Unit Properties section of this report details the different units and potential resources, concerns and issues associated with each.

Introduction

The following section briefly describes the regional geologic setting and the National Park Service Geologic Resource Evaluation Program.

Purpose of the Geologic Resource Evaluation Program

Geologic features and processes serve as the foundation of park ecosystems and an understanding of geologic resources yields important information for use in park decision making. The National Park Service Natural Resource Challenge, an action plan to advance the management and protection of park resources, has focused efforts to inventory the natural resources of parks. Ultimately, the inventory and monitoring of natural resources will become integral parts of park planning, operations and maintenance, visitor protection, and interpretation. The geologic component is carried out by the Geologic Resource Evaluation (GRE) Program administered by the NPS Geologic Resources Division. The goal of the GRE Program is to provide each of the identified 270 "Natural Area" parks with a digital geologic map, a geologic resource evaluation report, and a geologic bibliography. Each product is a tool to support the stewardship of park resources and is designed to be user friendly to non-geoscientists.

GRE teams hold scoping meetings at parks to review available data on the geology of a particular park and to discuss specific geologic issues affecting the park. Park staff are afforded the opportunity to meet with experts on the geology of their park during these meetings. Scoping meetings are usually held for individual parks although some meetings address an entire Vital Signs Monitoring Network.

Bedrock and surficial geologic maps and information provide the foundation for studies of groundwater, geomorphology, soils, and environmental hazards. Geologic maps describe the underlying physical habitat of many natural systems and are an integral component of the physical inventories stipulated by the National Park Service (NPS) in its Natural Resources Inventory and Monitoring Guideline (NPS-75) and the 1997 NPS Strategic Plan. The NPS GRE is a cooperative implementation of a systematic, comprehensive inventory of the geologic resources in National Park System units by the Geologic Resources Division, the Inventory, Monitoring, and Evaluation Office of the Natural Resource Program Center, the U.S. Geological Survey, and state geological surveys.

For additional information regarding the content of this report, please refer to the Geologic Resources Division of the National Park Service, located in Denver, Colorado with up-to-date contact information at the following website: http://www2.nature.nps.gov/geology/inventory/

Geologic Setting

Traveling across the High Plateau country of the Colorado Plateau, early explorers and settlers often came across cliff like edges that would "break" the relatively flat plateaus, resulting in time consuming, and often extremely dangerous detours. The juniper, known to the early settlers as "cedar," grew thick upon the plateaus; hence the name "Cedar Breaks."

Located in south- central Utah, Cedar Breaks National Monument encompasses about 6,155 acres of high desert landscape. The elevation in the park averages about 3,353 m (11,000 ft). The monument contains an erosional landscape modified by glacial and periglacial processes. The erosional amphitheatre of Cedar Breaks lies on the western rim of the Markagunt Plateau at 3,170 m (10,400 ft) elevation (figure 1). The Markagunt Plateau contains the highest elevations in southwestern Utah. A few miles north of Cedar Breaks, the basalt- capped Brianhead Peak reaches 3,449 m (11,315 ft) in elevation.

In the 1870s, Major John Wesley Powell began regional geological studies of the four corners area. One of the premier geologists with the Powell Survey, Clarence Dutton, recognized the Grand Staircase, a stair- step arrangement of cliff- forming rock layers that became progressively younger northward from the Grand Canyon (figure 3). The Tertiary- age Claron Formation that forms the majority of the rocks exposed at Cedar Breaks is one of the younger formations exposed in this Grand Staircase.

Over millions of years, sedimentary rocks of the Claron Formation and younger Tertiary rocks have been uplifted, eroded, and carved into a deep canyon that spans three miles and is over 2,000 feet deep. Cedar Breaks National Monument was set aside to preserve and protect an incredible collection of hoodoos. These fascinating geomorphological shapes include spires, fins, pinnacles, canyons, and mazes. The erosion of colorful sandstones, mudstones, and limestones left behind these fantastic remnants on the landscape. Erosional processes are also responsible for some of the management concerns at Cedar Breaks National Monument.

Cedar Breaks National Monument is located at the western margin of the Colorado Plateau, in the High Plateau region. The Colorado Plateau is a broad area of relative structural stability between the Rocky Mountains and the Basin and Range Physiographic Provinces.

The Colorado Plateau remains somewhat of a tectonic mystery and has undergone relatively little geologic deformation compared to the surrounding regions (Graham et al. 2002). It is roughly circular in shape, and extends about 483 km (300 miles) in an east- west direction and 644 km (400 miles) in the north- south direction. It ranges in altitude from about 762 m (2,500 ft) along the Colorado River, to about 3,962 m (13,000 ft) on some of the isolated peaks. The principal tectonic features of the plateau are basins, uplifts, monoclinal flexures, domes of igneous intrusion, platforms, slopes and broad saddles, and fold and fault belts (Kelley and Clinton 1960) (figure 2). Perhaps more than any other structural feature, the Colorado Plateau is characterized by monoclines, which, if lined up from end to end, would comprise an aggregate length of nearly 4,023 km (2,500 miles) (Kelley 1955). The term monocline, as defined by Powell in 1873, describes a bend or local steepening in otherwise gently inclined beds.

Surrounding Cedar Breaks are various uplifts, monoclines, and mountains. To the southwest, the Kaibab (monoclinal) Uplift dominates the area. The Circle Cliffs, Monument Uplift, and San Rafael Swell are to the northeast as are the Henry Mountains and the Miner's Mountain monocline. The Marysvale Volcanic Field borders the region on the north side. The Markagunt Plateau lies west of the Paunsaugunt Plateau that dominates Bryce Canyon National Park. It is at the edge of the High Plateaus province. To the east and northeast are the Table Cliff Plateau and the Kaiparowits Plateau, respectively.

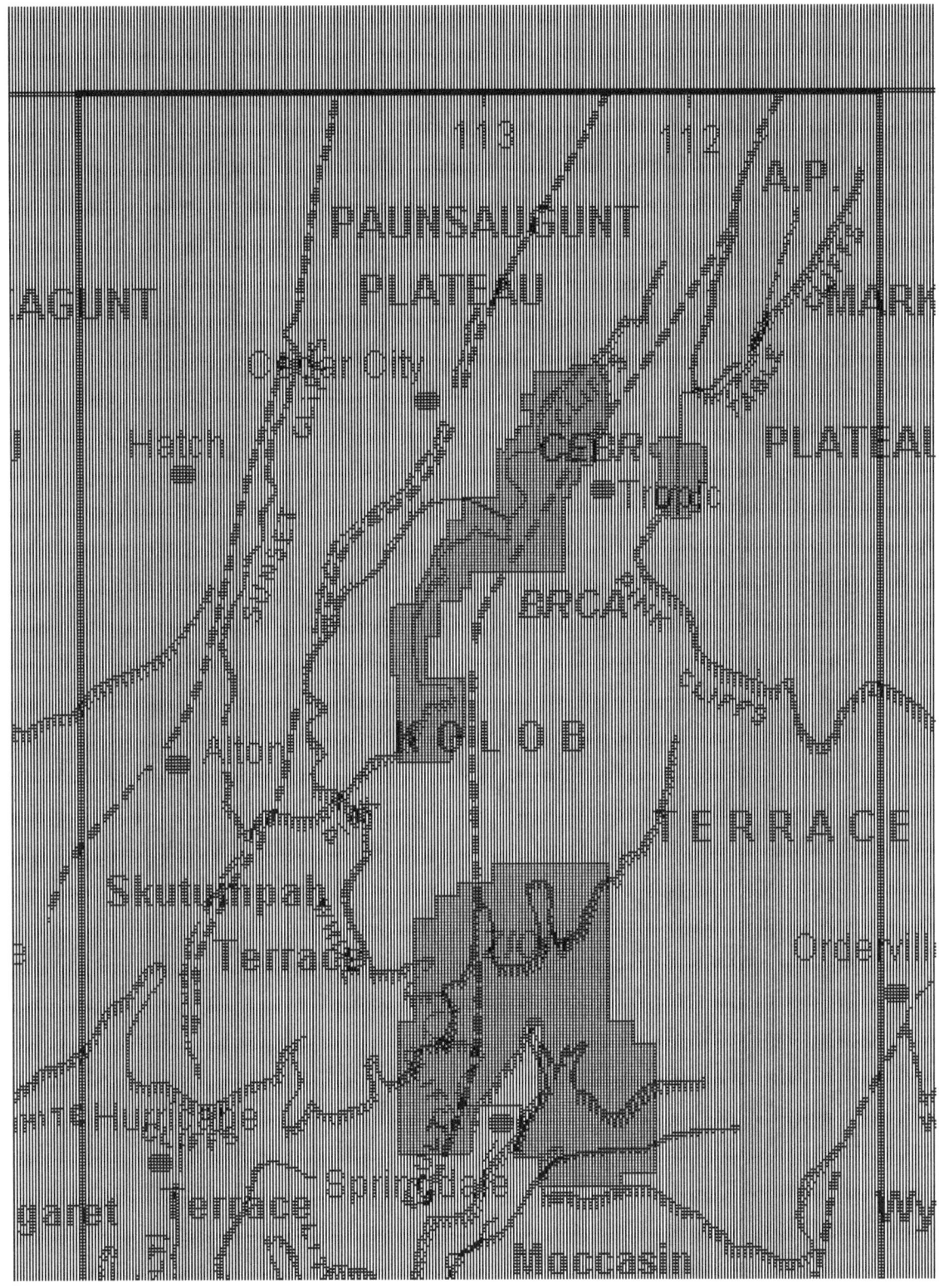

Figure 1. Location of Cedar Breaks National Monument relative to Zion National Park and Bryce Canyon National Park. Modified from Gregory (1950).

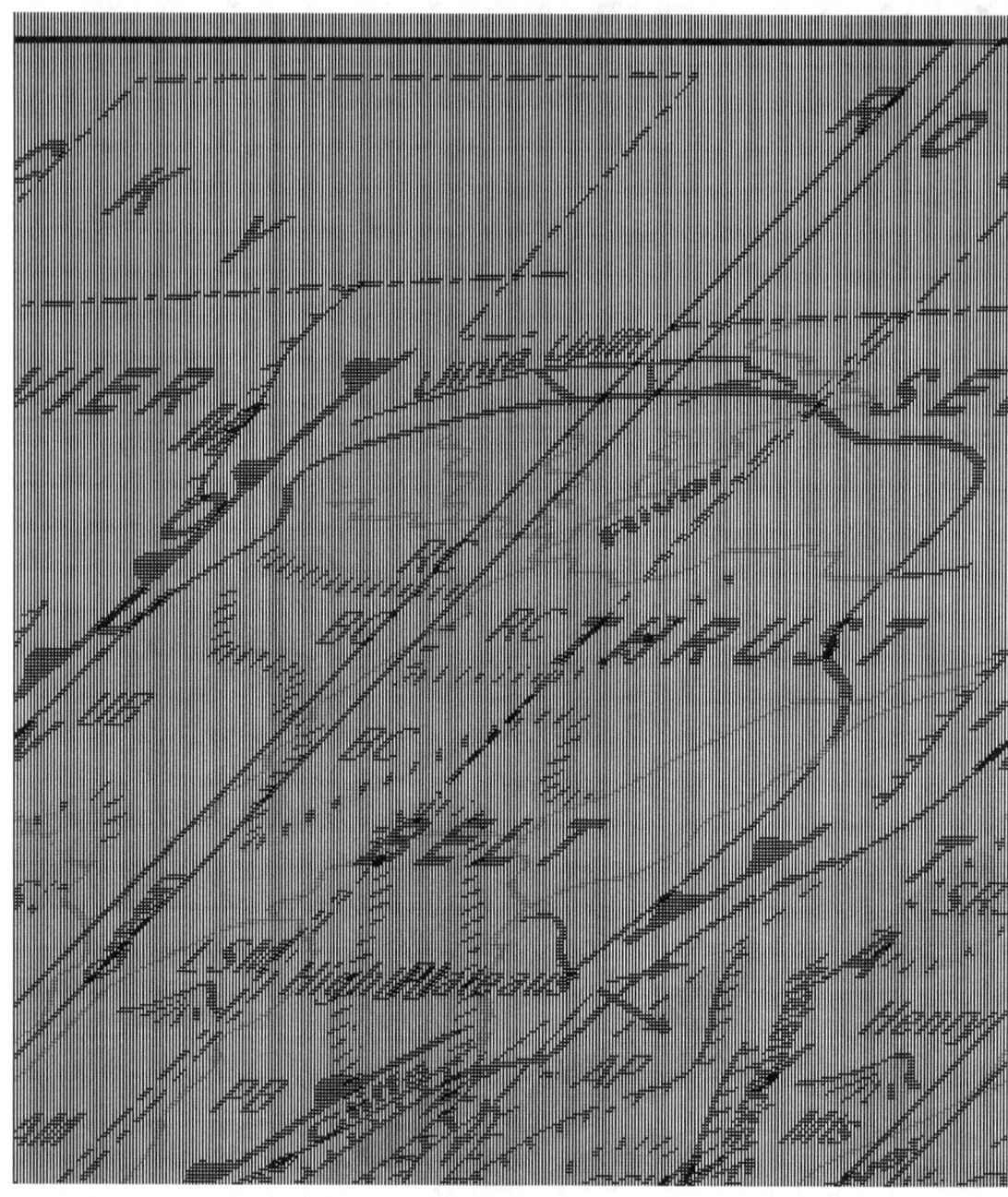

Figure 2. The Colorado Plateau, showing some of the significant uplifts, basins, faults, volcanic centers, and rivers. High areas are shown in gray: AM, Abajo Mts.; AP, Aquarius Plateau; BC, Book Cliffs; CCU, Circle Cliffs Uplift; DU, Defiance Uplift; KU, Kaibab Uplift; LSM, La Sal Mts.; MU, Monument Upwarp; RC, Roan Cliffs; SRS, San Rafael Swell; UU, Uncompahgre Uplift. Basins: PB, Paradox Basin; UB, Uinta Basin. Leading edge of Sevier Thrust Belt is shown as sawtooth with teeth on upper, overriding thrust plate. Modified from Kiver and Harris, 1999.

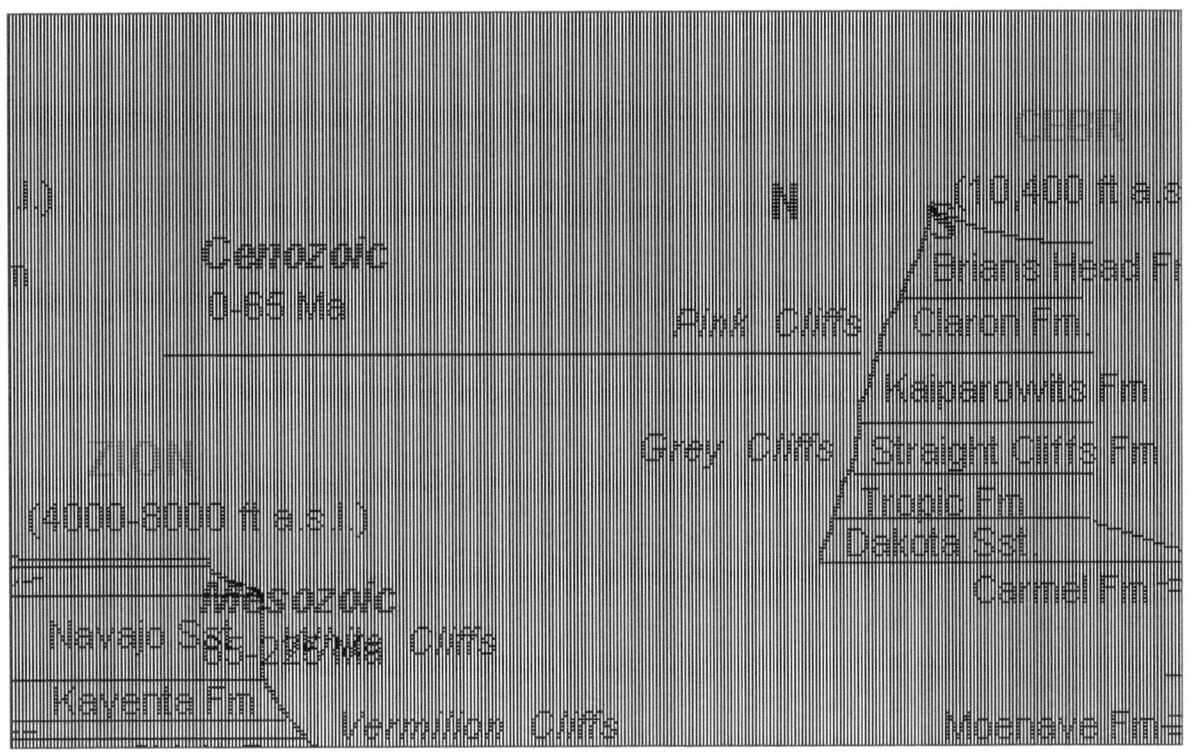

Figure 3. Geologic cross-section illustrating the "Grand Staircase" from the Grand Canyon to Bryce Canyon/Cedar Breaks. Rocks exposed as Cedar Breaks are colored yellow. "Ma": Millions of years ago; "Ba": billions of years ago. Modified from the geologic cross section published by the Zion Natural History Association, 1975.

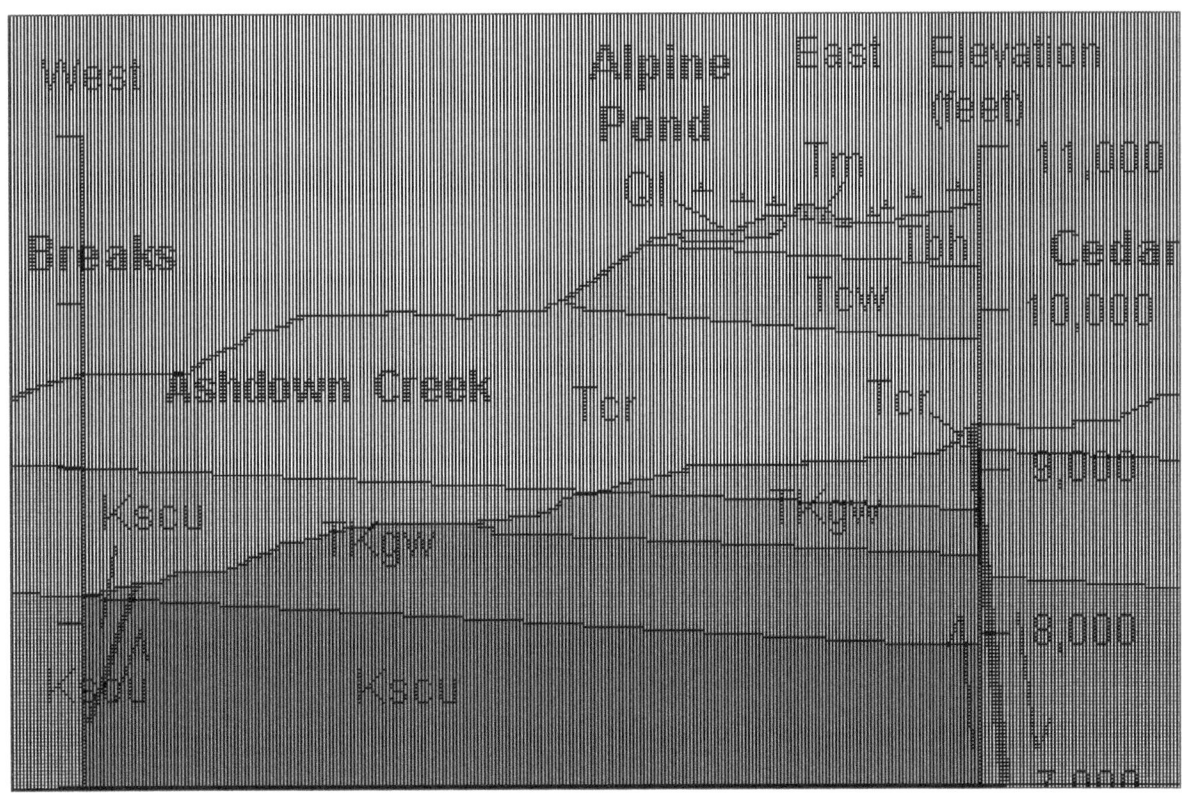

Figure 4. West to east geologic cross section through the central part of Cedar Breaks National Monument. Modified from Hatfield and others (2000).

Geologic Issues

A Geologic Resource Evaluation scoping session was held for Cedar Breaks National Monument July 15- 16, 1999, to discuss geologic resources, to address the status of geologic mapping, and to assess resource management issues and needs. The following section synthesizes the scoping results, in particular, those issues that may require attention from resource managers.

Slope Processes

Intense erosion of the relatively soft Tertiary Claron Formation is responsible for the vast array of hoodoos and canyons present at Cedar Breaks National Monument. However, erosional processes also are the cause of the most important geological resource management issues in the monument: landslides and rockfalls. Present and future construction and maintenance plans need to address fracturing and landslide (mass wasting) potential in the various formations listed as high risk in the Map Unit Properties section of this report.

Canyons and amphitheatres in Cedar Breaks have nearly vertical walls. This renders them highly dangerous because of the likelihood of rock falls, landslides, slumps, and slope creep. This issue is a major concern in the weaker rock units including the red member of the Claron Formation. Stronger rock units such as the White member of the Claron Formation and the Straight Cliffs Sandstone are highly fractured increasing the probability of rockfalls.

Slumps and other forms of slope failure are common for units that do not form cliffs. Unconsolidated alluvium, for example, is especially vulnerable to failure when exposed on a slope. Precipitation, which often produces flash flooding at Cedar Breaks, loosens rock and soil on slopes lacking stabilizing plant and tree roots. Rock and soil, when saturated with water, will slip down slope causing a slump, mudslide or debris flow. Landslide deposits have been mapped in Quaternary sediments, in the Markagunt Megabreccia, and in the Brian Head Formation. Quaternary landslide deposits (Ql) are identified on the geologic map.

New construction or routine maintenance work could trigger slope failure. If a road displaces the toe of a previous landslide, it could reactivate that landslide. Therefore, constructing roads, buildings, campgrounds, infrastructure, pipes, and water wells on landslide deposits and/or within the path of potential landslides should be avoided. Trails in the monument lead visitors through spectacular desert scenery; however, many of these trails are at high risk for rockfalls and landslides.

Inventory, Monitoring, and/or Research Needs for Slope Processes

- Perform a comprehensive study of the erosion processes active at Cedar Breaks National Monument, taking into account the different rock formations, slope aspects, location, and likelihood of instability.

- Create a rockfall susceptibility map using rock unit versus slope aspect in a GIS; use the map to plan future developments and aid current resource management of trails, buildings, and recreational use areas.

- Inventory and monitor debris flow potential near picnic areas; relate to slope and loose rock deposits. Possible methods for this type of monitoring range from simple stakes that can be located and monitored using periodic GPS measurements to high- tech continual laser readings.

- Inventory areas susceptible to flash floods and relate them to climate and flow patterns.

- Perform trail stability studies and determine which trails are most at risk and in need of further stabilization.

- Monitor areas planned for development for growth of fractures and for potential mass wasting.

- Study old landslides in detail to determine the amount of material moved, the cause of movement, the porosity and permeability of the landslide material, and the degree of saturation prior to movement. Also, inventory and document the slope angle and the impacts of mass movements.

Seismicity and Mining

The Basin and Range and Colorado Plateau are still seismically active. Minor earthquakes occur in Nevada and Utah almost daily, most too small to be detected without a seismometer. The Wasatch Front, north of Cedar Breaks, near Salt Lake City, is due for a major earthquake. No historical earthquakes associated with surface rupture have occurred along the Wasatch fault zone during at least the past 133 years. However, the recurrence interval, or time between major seismic events, for the entire Wasatch fault zone may be 50 to 430 years (Swan et al. 1980). The Hurricane fault zone underlies the western scarp of the Markagunt Plateau. This fault zones is one of the major displacement areas within the Basin and Range, accommodating at least 3,050 m (10,000 ft) of movement in the Cedar City area. This fault and other local normal faults within and to the west of Cedar Breaks National Monument are still considered seismically active. Washington, Utah, near St. George, experienced a magnitude 5.9 earthquake in 1992 (Hatfield et al. 2000). Most of the faults within the monument are north to northeast trending and small-scale with less than 30 m (100 ft) of displacement.

Several mines that use blasting to extract ore, coal, and other resources are located near Cedar Breaks National Monument. Blasting creates seismic waves that propagate through the earth, resulting in surface vibration.

The delicate hoodoos of Cedar Breaks National Monument are largely the reason the area was set aside for preservation and protection. Severe ground shaking from either natural or man- made sources, has a great impact on the geomorphology of Cedar Breaks and is considered a significant resource management issue.

Inventory, Monitoring, and/or Research Needs for Seismicity and Mining

- Perform a comprehensive study of the faulting and seismic processes active at Cedar Breaks National Monument, taking into account rock formations, slope aspects, location and likelihood of instability.
- Monitor slopes along trails particularly in areas prone to fail in the event of seismic activity in the area.
- Develop a visitor access plan to avoid areas beneath the rim of the canyons to avoid rockfalls.
- Monitor seismic activity in the Cedar Breaks area by cooperating with local agencies including the USGS and Utah Geological Survey.
- Determine the effects of nearby mining, including blasting, on the delicate features at Cedar Breaks. How does this relate to natural seismicity in the area?
- Perform a comprehensive study of the seismicity of active faults in close proximity to Cedar Breaks area including the mapping of small- scale faults and shear fractures.

Karst and fracturing within the Claron Formation

Fracturing in the Claron Formation is a geological process that has the potential to disrupt the stability and safety of visitor overlooks. Increased erosion from fracture failure and landsliding (mass wasting) also pose potential problems for the resource manager. The Brian Head Formation, Markagunt Megabreccia, and unconsolidated Quaternary sediments have the highest risk of failure by mass wasting.

Sinkholes, seeps, springs, and other karst- related features have also developed in the Tertiary Claron Formation. Sinkhole development may impact new and existing construction. Caves associated with springs may yield cultural artifacts, including dwellings, tools, and petroglyphs.

Inventory, Monitoring, and/or Research Needs for Karst and Fracturing within the Claron Formation

- Perform a comprehensive inventory of the fractures in the Claron Formation and develop a plan to monitor any change in the fractures including photo-documentation and measurements of fractures.
- Inventory sinkholes and areas that are likely to develop sinkholes.
- Inventory caves in the monument.

- Perform detailed studies of the Claron and Brian Head Formations along with cataloging the geological features of Cedar Breaks National Monument using a Global Positioning System and GIS. These studies would also help in monitoring rates of erosion and weathering.

Water Issues

Water is principally responsible for the formation of the various rock shapes at Cedar Breaks, and continues to play a critical role in sculpting the landscape. Rain at Cedar Breaks often occurs as locally torrential showers. The intensity of rain in a country almost barren of soil and vegetation results in severe erosion (Gregory and Moore 1931). Intense rain events falling on unprotected soil knocks apart individual soil particles and washes unconsolidated sediment into the canyons.

Rainwater combines with carbon dioxide in the atmosphere to form carbonic acid (H_2CO_3). Although a weak acid, over time carbonic acid effectively dissolves limestone in rock layers and in intergranular cement. Lindquist (1980) discovered that the freeze and thaw action of water on the rocks at nearby Bryce Canyon National Park was perhaps the most effective weathering process.

Numerous small springs forming where the ground surface intersects an aquifer or groundwater conduit, are especially common along very steep slopes. The two types of springs in the Cedar Breaks area are alluvial and bedrock springs. Alluvial springs are formed by water pockets near the surface in unconsolidated sediments. Much deeper are bedrock springs which originate from flow along fractures and bedding planes within lithified rock.

Water, though integral, is scarce on the Markagunt Plateau, as it is for southern Utah in general. Much of the water used at the park comes from wells, penetrating the surface to reach aquifers in the Claron Formation, Wahweap and Straight Cliffs Sandstones. Aquifers must be deep enough to be relatively impervious to drought and occur in fractured rock to provide groundwater conduits to the well.

Inventory, Monitoring, and/or Research Needs for Water Issues

- Determine the nature of the watershed of the monument by compiling baseline watershed data, and surface and subsurface hydrogeologic data, including discharge rates of surface water.
- Monitor water quality on a multiple sample location basis within the park; drinking water sources are especially important.
- Perform hydrogeologic studies of the groundwater and surface water systems to better define groundwater flow, and the association of groundwater with karst and cave development.
- Study groundwater flow patterns. A drinking water supply and low water use alternatives for waste disposal are two significant issues for Cedar Breaks;

knowledge of groundwater flow patterns and alternative waste technologies would be beneficial to the resource manager.

- Research the effects of a forest canopy on surface water availability. How does it impact the water supply and the ecosystem as a whole?
- Install additional wells for testing and drinking water.
- Study the impacts of nearby mining operations on the hydrology of the area (see above mining issues discussion).
- Identify and study potential sources of groundwater for quality.
- Install transducers and data loggers in wells.
- Investigate additional methods to characterize groundwater recharge areas and flow directions.
- Study groundwater recharge mechanisms and shallow subsurface flow in carbonate terrains in the southern Utah.
- Conduct a study of aquifer permeability and of the quantity of water present in Cedar Breaks National Monument.

Ecosystems and Cultural Resources

Inventory, Monitoring, and/or Research Needs for Ecosystems and Cultural Resources

- Study the fire history of bogs for the last 20,000 years. Lowder Creek can be traced back 17,000 years, Red Valley 11,000 years, and Alpine Pond 3,000 years.
- Monitor and inventory human impacts in the park, including cultural resources.
- Research chert distribution around the monument. The distribution of chert has numerous cultural implications.
- Develop a better understanding of the relationship between clustered vegetation and bedrock strata.
- Determine the relationship between geology and archeology by studying dune and mud deposits on the rim.

Hoodoo Formation and Present Condition

Preserving and maintaining hoodoos and other landforms in their natural environment is a key resource management issue for Cedar Breaks National Monument. The relationship between rock units and erosional processes is a dynamic one. Changes in climate, especially precipitation, have a profound effect on the entire system. Determining the balance between visitor access and feature preservation is a difficult task.

Inventory, Monitoring, and/or Research Needs for Hoodoo Formation and Present Condition

- Study the progressive evolution of hoodoos; examine morphology and internal stratigraphy and structure for interpretive value.
- Study the impact of solution weathering and freeze-thaw cycles on fractures.

- Study the responses of different lithologies to weathering and erosion.
- Study processes affecting landscape evolution including: rates of edge migration, erosion, retreat of rim, rates of down cutting of streams at the bottom of canyons, and aggradation of bottom fill.
- Study and monitor atmospheric conditions with respect to the hydrology of the park.
- Perform a detailed 3- dimensional cartographic survey of the Markagunt Plateau.
- Study hoodoo fluting to determine if it is vertical or follows bedding.

Paleontologic Potential

The desert landscape of Cedar Breaks contains more than just hoodoos; it contains a record of prolific ancient life. Fossils found in geologic formations exposed within or near the monument include corals, gastropods (snails), pelecypod bivalves (clams, oysters), vertebrates (fish, turtles, dinosaurs, birds, and mammals), plants, and petrified wood.

The Upper Cretaceous Straight Cliffs Formation is known to have fossil wood and plant fragments (Hatfield et al. 2000 a, b). Thin beds of fossiliferous limestones contain oysters and are found in lower beds of the Straight Cliffs Formation in Cedar Canyon (Hatfield et al. 2000 a, b). Vertebrate fossils including fish, turtles, and dinosaurs were collected from the Straight Cliffs Formation just west of Cedar Breaks (Hatfield et al. 2000 a, b; Eaton et al. 1999a). Fossil pelecypods, vertebrates, leaf fragments and carbonized wood are locally found in the Upper Cretaceous Wahweap Sandstone and Upper Cretaceous- Paleocene(?) Grand Castle Formation. The Paleocene- Eocene Claron Formation is poorly fossiliferous although a few pelecypods and gastropods have been found (Hatfield et al. 2000 a, b). Bown and others (1997) also collected some insect trace fossils from the Claron Formation. The lower "variegated" unit of the Eocene- Oligocene Brian Head Formation has vertebrate fauna including bony fish, ray teeth, and abundant turtle fossils 30 miles northeast of Cedar Breaks (Eaton et al. 1999b). A ray, an unidentified bird, an alligator, and ungulate fossils were also collected as were teeth from marsupials and rodents. Quaternary insects, plant macrofossils, spores and pollen have been recovered from pond deposits adjacent to Cedar Breaks and radiocarbon dated to 17,000 years bp (Santucci, 2000). Specimens found within Cedar Breaks should be protected and catalogued for scientific study, and preserved for future generations to enhance visitor appreciation of the entire monument.

Inventory, Monitoring, and/or Research Needs for Paleontological Potential

- Perform a comprehensive study of the paleontologic resources at Cedar Breaks National Monument focusing on Cretaceous, Paleocene, Eocene, and Oligocene rocks to determine if fossils are present in backcountry areas.

- Inventory all paleontologic specimens collected in the monument. If possible, determine the locations of specimens removed from the monument that are in private collections.
- Determine localities from which fossils were found, document localities, fill out paleontology locality forms, and conduct condition assessment to meet GPRA goal 1A9
- Interpret the fossil resources of Cedar Breaks using graphics, brochures, and exhibits. Stress the scientific importance of fossils and the need to protect and preserve fossil resources.
- Develop appropriate paleontological resource monitoring strategies to facilitate scientific research, visitor interpretation, and resource management of park fossils.
- Caves sinkholes and springs (such as Arch Springs Cave) in the Claron Formation may preserve paleontological material, although none is currently known. Further investigation is recommended to determine their paleontological potential (Santucci et al. 2001).

Faulting and Deformation Processes

Rocks at Cedar Breaks have undergone multiple phases of deformation resulting in folds, faults, joints and other fractures compromising the strength of rock units and impacting many of the features in the monument. For instance, faults and fractures can focus surface runoff and by erosion, eventually widen them into gullies. When parallel gullies are separated by a jointed rock unit, water follows the joints, eroding the rock and ultimately separating spires from the rest of the column. Deformation is an active and on going process at Cedar Breaks. Rocks, being somewhat brittle, respond to pressure by developing small- scale fractures and joints. Understanding the nature of deformation allows geologists to identify areas of weakness in rock where weathering and erosion are the greatest. Identifying these areas is of importance to a resource manager.

Inventory, Monitoring, and/or Research Needs for Faulting and Deformation Processes

- Study the role of jointing versus faulting (both strike- slip and thrust faulting) in the evolution of the landscape.
- Study the Markagunt Megabreccia (breccia is a rock, composed of cemented rock fragments as a result of fracturing, often found in fault zones) near Cedar Breaks for regional tectonic implications.
- Conduct an inventory of all recent fault scarps in the area, commonly present in surficial Quaternary deposits.

Mining Issues

Interest in uranium mining in the area peaked following World War II. The principal host rocks for uranium exposed near Cedar Breaks are the Triassic Chinle Formation and the Jurassic Morrison Formation.

Abandoned mines pose a threat to an ecosystem and to the health and safety of visitors. Surface water and groundwater can be contaminated by high concentrations of heavy metals leached from the mine itself and from mine tailings. Heavy metals may also contaminate nearby soils, which in turn can impact plant and animal life that live in the soil. Another threat specific to uranium mining is that of radon gas exposure. Radon is a tasteless, odorless gas produced by the radioactive decay of uranium. Radon is a known carcinogen that usually concentrates in low- lying areas like basements and mineshafts.

Coal beds are present in the strata of Cedar Breaks. Coal indicates that swamps and bogs covered the landscape in the past. There are 22 coalfields in Utah found primarily in Cretaceous strata such as the Straight Cliffs Formation. The major coalfields contain more than a billion tons of coal. In southwest Utah, these include the Alton, Kaiparowits, and Kolob coalfields, which account for over 95 percent of the coal resources in Utah. Minor coalfields account for approximately 4 percent of the total (State of Utah 2004).

Cedar Breaks NM has been withdrawn from federal mineral leasing laws and the mining law of 1872 governing mining claims, therefore exploration and exploitation of coal and oil and gas is not possible within the monument. However, mineral development in the area surrounding Cedar Breaks may pose a threat to the viewshed and ecosystem of the monument. Since the cost of mining coal is directly affected by transportation costs, proximity to existing roads and railroads greatly influences the siting of coalmines (State of Utah 2004). Coal mining and oil and gas production often results in new road construction, water pollution, noise, and a local population increase. The Surface Mining Control and Reclamation Act of 1977 contains specific provisions protecting park units from the affects of surface coal mining adjacent to park boundaries.

Inventory, Monitoring, and/or Research Needs for Mining Resources and Issues

- Maintain awareness of the potential encroachment of oil and gas exploration and potential surface coal mining adjacent to of the park.
- Perform a thorough investigation of uranium occurrence in the monument. This should include descriptions of uranium bearing rock units, uranium content analysis, and an inventory of locations where beds are exposed at the surface and are accessible to the public.
- Complete an inventory of the uranium content of recent unconsolidated deposits and soils as well as the uranium bearing stratigraphic units. Assess the impacts of uranium on fauna and flora in the monument
- Acquire plugging records of oil and gas wells potentially connected to park groundwater systems.
- Conduct periodic surface and ground water sampling as well as soil sampling for uranium. Monitoring the mineral content of drinking water is chiefly important.

Marysvale Volcanic Field

Bounding Cedar Breaks to the north is the locally extensive Marysvale Volcanic Field. This field formed when local extension allowed molten rock to rise through the earths crust and penetrate the surface with flows and small- scale cones. The volcanic field is contemporaneous with other volcanic features on the Colorado Plateau including Capulin Volcano. In addition to lava flows in the area, the volcanic field spewed vast blankets of ash over the landscape that are preserved in the youngest rocks at Cedar Breaks today.

Inventory, Monitoring, and/or Research Needs for Marysvale Volcanic Field

- Date the appropriate minerals applicable to age dating lava flows.

- Determine the amount of volcanic material originally present in the monument and how much has been subsequently removed by erosion.

- Use resistivity to locate cavities in flows. Cavities, including lava tubes and large vesicles, may contain preserved animals.

- Conduct a detailed study of fractures, faults, and bedding within the area.

- Conduct detailed mapping of volcanic features in the volcanic field.

Wind Erosion and Deposition

In addition to water, wind is a major force that can redistribute soil and soil resources (e.g., litter, organic matter, and nutrients) within and among ecosystems. Erosion and deposition by wind is important at Cedar Breaks National Monument and can be accelerated by human activities.

Accelerated losses of soil and soil biota by erosion may indicate a degradation of the ecosystem. Ecosystem health is dependent on the retention of these resources. In addition, wind erosion and sediment transport may be strongly impacted by land- use practices outside the monument. Because monument management practices limit or prohibit off- road travel, human impacts within the monument are primarily associated with off- trail hiking in high- use areas. Where livestock grazing or trailing is still permitted, accelerated soil erosion can be more extensive.

Inventory, Monitoring, and/or Research Needs for Wind Erosion and Deposition

- Monitor movement of soil materials.

- Investigate the consequences of soil movement on the ecosystem.

- Investigate the natural range of soil movement in relation to landscape configuration and characteristics.

General Geology

This report is an attempt to further the long- term goal of improving the understanding of geologic processes at Cedar Breaks by providing suggestions for future work and baseline information, including the attached digital geologic map of the park. However, for the scientific community and the general public, the geology of Cedar Breaks National Monument offers many opportunities to further the knowledge of desert erosional processes, geologic history, and ancient Native American cultures.

Inventory, Monitoring, and/or Research Needs for General Geology

- Perform rock color studies.

- Identify stratigraphic packages bounded by unconformities in order to better define past depositional systems.

- Continue to study and implement geographic information systems (GIS) technology for interpretation, resource management, and maintenance. This can be done through interpretive mapping, 3- D visualization, virtual field trips, and rockfall hazard assessments (McNeil et al. 2002).

- Obtain GIS data for the unique geologic features of Cedar Breaks and catalog these features using a Global Positioning System (GPS). This project would also allow for future monitoring of erosion associated with specific features.

- Study the glacial and megabreccia deposits around Brian Head Peak. Questions remain regarding the origin and deposition of the megabreccia. Hatfield and others (2000) have addressed some of these questions.

- Develop educational brochures, graphics and outreach programs about the geology of Cedar Breaks, emphasizing its unique location relative to the transition zone between the Colorado Plateau and Basin and Range physiographic provinces.

Geologic Features and Processes

This section provides descriptions of the most prominent and distinctive geologic features and processes in Cedar Breaks National Monument.

Markagunt Megabreccia

The Markagunt Megabreccia is exposed in the eastern part of Cedar Breaks National Monument. One of several large structurally emplaced units in the southern High Plateaus, the Markagunt Megabreccia has a measured thickness ranging from 5 to 130 feet at Blowhard Mountain, southeast of the monument, and in surrounding areas (Hatfield et al. 2000).

The Markagunt Megabreccia was originally thought to have been emplaced by repeated landsliding along these slip surfaces following tectonic uplift of the Markagunt Plateau. However, this interpretation became suspect because only Brian Head Mountain rises topographically above the breccia in the area and Brian Head is 6 miles from the megabreccia at Blowhard Mountain.

Slip surfaces responsible for the creation of the Markagunt Megabreccia occur mainly in the Brian Head Formation. Other slip surfaces are in the Bear Valley Formation and the Mount Dutton Formation. Both the Brian Head Formation and Bear Valley Formation are poorly lithified and contain high amounts of volcanic ash, making them lithologically and structurally unstable units. Slip surfaces in the Mount Dutton Formation are in a mudstone breccia unit.

Typically, landslides are incapable of traveling 6 miles. Furthermore, if a landslide had come from the Brian Head peak area it would contain clasts of the Leach Canyon Formation, which is exposed on the peak. However, Leach Canyon clasts do not occur in the megabreccia. Hatfield and others (2000) hypothesize that the Markagunt Megabreccia was emplaced by gravity induced sliding along stratigraphically controlled slip surfaces and that this formation once covered Cedar Breaks, Blowhard Mountain, and areas at least several miles farther south. Testing of this hypothesis continues today.

Hypotheses concerning the causes of the gravity sliding also remain to be tested. One hypothesis states that sliding was the result of the emplacement of a large batholith that caused uplift of the Markagunt Plateau. Another suggests that the megabreccia slid off a structural dome caused by the emplacement of the Iron Peak laccolith located about 15 miles north-northeast of Cedar Breaks. A third hypothesis proposes emplacement of the megabreccia by gravity sliding off outward penetrating thrust sheets generated by the weight and collapse of the Marysvale volcanic field to the north (Hatfield et al. 2000). More research is needed to test these hypotheses.

Structural Features

Figure 4 illustrates the gently eastward dip of the Markagunt Plateau. The Markagunt Plateau is a fault block that has been uplifted and tilted along faults within the Hurricane Fault Zone. The Hurricane Fault Zone is a major fault zone in Utah with normal fault displacement of at least 3,000 m (10,000 feet) in the Cedar City area (Hatfield et al. 2000). The Hurricane Fault Zone is an example of late Cenozoic basin and range deformation caused by extensional tectonics. After millions of years of compressive tectonics during the Paleozoic and Mesozoic Eras, this was an episode of extensional deformation involving the southwestern North American margin.

Compression resulted from the collision of lithospheric plates expressed by thrusting as in the Sevier Orogeny deforming only near-surface sedimentary strata. Reverse faulting as in the Laramide Orogeny, involved Precambrian metamorphic and igneous rocks, as well. These tectonic events were the result of complex plate tectonic movements along the western seaboard of North America.

The High Plateau country of the Colorado Plateau contains evidence of both basin and range normal faulting and reverse faulting although only normal faults have been mapped at Cedar Breaks National Monument. The number of faults and the amount of displacement along these faults decreases across the High Plateau region into the main part of the Colorado Plateau. In Cedar Breaks, the normal faults trend north to northeast and have displacements of generally less than 100 feet (Hatfield et al. 2000). Movement along the Hurricane Fault may have begun about 10 million years ago and continues today as evidenced by the 1992, 5.9 magnitude (local magnitude) earthquake near the town of Washington, Utah.

Erosion of the landscape

Multicolored cliffs, spires, pinnacles, and other unique features at Cedar Breaks were carved by erosion, weathering, and mass wasting on the western edge of the Markagunt Plateau. Headward erosion of the Ashdown Creek drainage cutting into the rim of the Markagunt Plateau created much of the topography we see today. The freezing and thawing of water in fractures and joints breaks rock down by acting as a wedge to pry the rocks apart. Chemical alteration and dissolution of the minerals in the rock due to percolating groundwater or surface water has carved out intricate steps in the Claron Formation. With intense rainstorms, weakened and loosened rocks move downslope either by gravity alone (e.g., talus at the base of cliffs) or by sheetwash and flash flooding.

Rivers on the Colorado Plateau cut through essentially horizontal sedimentary rocks, creating steep cliffs and terraces. Resistant rocks such as the Claron Formation cap the plateau and overly the softer formations. The underlying less resistant rocks are eroded back under the lip of the cap rock. Eventually, erosion removes enough of the underlying material that the cap rock collapses, moving the cliff face ever backward. The rate of cliff face retreat at Cedar Breaks is astonishing. This rapid retreat is attributed to several factors: 1) the rate of weathering is high, 2) the amount of protective vegetative cover is low, 3) the erosion of soft rocks is rapid, and 4) the rapid undercutting of the red limestone member of the Claron Formation where the white limestone member acts as a cap rock (Lindquist 1980).

Hoodoo Formation

This erosional process is responsible for the formation of hoodoos at Cedar Breaks. Hoodoos are formed when more resistant rock acts as a cap on top of less resistant rock forming a column, pinnacle or pillar of rock. The formation of hoodoos is in part a function of joints and fractures, which accelerates the erosion process. The trends of walls and ridges found in Cedar Breaks closely follow the trends of the dominant joints within the intact rock units (Brox 1961).

Jointing is not the only control on hoodoo formation, especially if the rock is not hard and competent. This absence joint control is thought to result from the combination of weak beds and the overall rapid rate of wall retreat. Because of the extremely high rates of erosional retreat and bedrock weathering, it is unlikely that the joints offer much added weakness. Hoodoos tend to form on the crest of ridges between gullies in the red limestone member of the Claron Formation near the head of the escarpment.

Separating the hoodoo from the gully slopes are sharp weathering transitions from rapid slope weathering to the much slower weathering of the bedrock surfaces (Lindquist 1980). Any hoodoo formation in the slope-forming member is thus a self-enhancing mechanism (Engineers International Inc. 1980). The presence of sedimentary layers of alternating resistance to erosion appears to be crucial in hoodoo development. This variation and alternation of resistant layers is a primary feature of the Claron Formation (Lindquist, 1980).

As in nearby Bryce Canyon National Park, the pinnacles of Cedar Breaks vary in height from less than 12 m (40 ft) to 61 m (200 ft) or more. The eroded limestone forms an intricate landscape of arches, spires, pinnacles, and natural bridges (Engineers International, Inc. 1980). Some hoodoos extend from the escarpment at right angles and are like walls. Lindquist (1980) called these "primary hoodoos." Secondary hoodoos extend at various angles from primary hoodoos or slopes leading to primary hoodoos. Ridge hoodoos form on ridge crests some distance (100's of meters) from the primary escarpment. Hoodoos can form complexes as clusters of shapes with a radiating configuration.

Other Features

- The tapestry of colors is another feature that contributes to the unique appearance of the monument. Although the exact coloring agents in the rock still need to be identified, the colors are currently believed to be due to various amounts of iron and manganese compounds (Hatfield et al. 2000).

- Cedar Breaks is a unique location on the Colorado Plateau where a visitor has a splendid view of the Basin and Range landscape to the west while standing on a plateau of nearly flat-lying rock layers. This transition in structure and topographic expression from one geologic province to another is further illustrated by the variety of volcanic and sedimentary rock units derived from various source areas on the Colorado Plateau.

Map Unit Properties

This section provides a description for and identifies many characteristics of the map units that appear on the digital geologic map of Cedar Breaks National Monument. The table is highly generalized and is provided for informational purposes only. Ground disturbing activities should not be permitted or denied on the basis of information contained in this table. More detailed unit descriptions can be found in the help files that accompany the digital geologic map or by contacting the NPS Geologic Resources Division.

Mesozoic rocks underlie Cedar Breaks National Monument almost entirely. Capping the high points are Tertiary and Quaternary rocks. Because of intense erosion, these rocks are on striking display.

The Upper Cretaceous Straight Cliffs Formation, the oldest formation in Cedar Breaks, is derived from a mixture of sand, mud, limy ooze, and organic matter which lithified into a coal- rich unit. The sandstones, mudstones, and siltstones of the Grand Castle and Wahweap Sandstones followed this deposition.

The Tertiary Claron Formation is the result of local basins filling with sediments. The Brian Head Formation was deposited over the Claron. Erosion of these units during uplift formed the spindly hoodoos, amphitheatres, klippes, and other fantastic geomorphological shapes discussed above.

Volcanic eruptions throughout the area are responsible for the tuffaceous layers of the Oligocene Isom Formation and Miocene Leach Canyon Formations. The mysterious, intensely deformed, chaotic mass of the Markagunt Megabreccia, also of Miocene age, lies above the tuff deposits preceding another volcanic event. This event left basalt and other mafic lava flows in the area. Pleistocene glaciation and other geomorphological agents, such as streams and landslides, have left recent Quaternary age deposits on the landscape of Cedar Breaks National Monument.

The following table presents the stratigraphic column of Cedar Breaks and an itemized list of features associated with each map unit. This table lists the properties specific to each unit including: map symbol, name, description, resistance to erosion, suitability for development, hazards, potential paleontologic resources, cultural and mineral resources, potential karst issues, potential recreational use, and global significance.

For further information on map units and other ancillary map information, please consult the Windows help file: CEBRGLG.hlp (included on CD).

Map Unit Properties Table

Age	Unit Name (Symbol)	Features and Description	Erosion Resistance	Suitability for Development	Hazards	Potential Paleontologic Resources	Potential Cultural Resources	Potential for Karst	Mineral Resources & Specimens	Habitat	Recreation Potential	Global Significance
Quaternary	Artificial fill (af)	Man-made fill deposits, mostly for dams and highways										
Quaternary	Alluvium (Qal), alluvial-terrace deposits (Qalb), sheetwash alluvium (Qac), colluvium (Qc), Volcanic gravel colluvium (Qcv), peat (Qo), eolian deposits (Qes), landslide deposits (Qms), alluvial fan deposits (Qf), older talus and colluvium (Qmt2), older alluvium (Qa2), and older landslide deposits (QTl)	Unconsolidated sediments deposited in eolian, alluvial, fan, and landslides; includes peat deposits. Pleistocene and Holocene landslide deposits (Qms), colluvium (Qc), alluvial fans (Qf), and alluvium (Qal) are common in CEBR (Hatfield et al., 2000). Landslides in the Brian Head Formation are especially common. Alpine Pond fills a depression formed by a landslide, and about 50 feet of Isom Fm. blocks are exposed along the landslide scarp above the pond. Peat (Qo) has formed from Pleistocene and Holocene bog deposits that occur in and near the monument. Vegetation has stabilized eolian dunes (Qes) just east of the Cedar Breaks rim (Hatfield et al., 2000).	Low to very low	Units are suitable for most development unless exposed on a slope where unconsolidated deposits are prone to fail. High permeability of units makes some waste facility development problematic. Presence of any altered volcanics (as swelling clays) may make road and trail development risky.	High landslide potential as well as mass wasting, especially when units are water saturated.	Local fossil remains; many likely washed in from other units	Tools, arrowheads and other artifacts	None	Sand and gravel	Forms valley fill throughout monument	Suitable for most recreation including hiking, biking, camping	Quaternary peat deposits
Quaternary	Basalt (Qb), and olivine-plagioclase mafic volcanic rock lava flows (Qbfi)	Black & gray, vesicular, generally crystalline poor, basalt. Some units with visible crystals of olivine and plagioclase present as lava flows. Resistant basalt forms lava flows, flow breccia, dikes, and cinder cones just east of CEBR; vegetated flows probably Pleistocene in age; those without vegetation may be Holocene.	Moderate to high	Units are suitable for most development unless high fracture density is present. Any altered clays, associated with the volcanics may lead to unstable road, trail, and building foundations.	Rockfall potential when exposed on a cliff face.	None	None documented	None	Olivine plagioclase and clinopyroxene phenocrysts	Vugs and vesides, if large enough, can provide habitat	Suitable for most recreation.	Potential for data modern volcanics
Tertiary (Miocene)	Markagunt Megabreccia (Tm)	Angular clasts and broken masses of Brian Head, Wah Wah Springs (not in CEBR), Isom, Bear Valley, and Mount Dutton (not in CEBR) Formations form the poorly exposed, structurally chaotic assemblage of Markagunt Megabreccia; rock masses, house- to city-block- sized, set in a matrix of sheared and folded rocks of same units. Some masses are as large as 1 square mile. 20- 46 m (65-150 ft) thick.	Low	Most permanent development on this unit is not recommended due to the highly fractured nature of the breccia.	Rockfall and landslide potential high; highly fractured and deformed unit.	Fragments from other units	None documented	None	Boulders and other landscaping materials; Fascinating deformed rock	Fractured nature of unit lends to many cavities for nests and burrows	Recreation not recommended due to deformed nature of unit	Large gravity slide deposits, type locality
Tertiary (Miocene)	Leach Canyon Formation (Tl)	The distinctive, rhyolite ash- flow tuffs of Miocene age (23.8 Ma); cooling units may be associated with the Caliente caldera complex straddling Nevada- Utah border about 60 miles to the west. Leach Canyon tuffs did not extend past eastern section of the Markagunt Plateau. Phenocrysts make up about 10 to 20 % of the crystal- poor tuff; ubiquitous brownish-red rhyolite lithic clasts, rounded gas cavities lined with yellow vapor- phase minerals, and abundant white collapsed pumice fragments; 26 m (85 ft) thick.	Moderate	Poorly welded; friable and weak for road & buildings foundations, trails and camp sites; variable permeability may allow waste facility development.	Highly friable; easily eroded; slides and slumping probable.	None	None documented	None	Zeolite minerals in vugs, tuffs; volcanic glass; pumice and other volcanic rocks	Vugs and vesicles, if large enough can provide habitat	Suitable for most recreation except rock climbing and other types dependent on slope stability	23.8 Ma tuff layer

Age	Unit Name (Symbol)	Features and Description	Erosion Resistance	Suitability for Development	Hazards	Potential Paleontologic Resources	Potential Cultural Resources	Potential for Karst	Mineral Resources & Specimens	Habitat	Recreation Potential	Global Significance
Tertiary (Oligocene)	Isom Formation (Ti)	Three members: the Blue Meadows Tuff member, Baldhills Tuff member (may be 650 feet thick), and Hole-in-the-Wall Tuff member. North of CEBR, Baldhills Tuff member forms at least three cooling units totaling about 80 feet thick; units consist of dark gray, black, and brick red tuff with long linear vesicles and local breccia; formation generally composed of resistant, reddish-brown to dark gray, crystal-poor, densely welded, trachytic ash-flow tuffs; 24 m (80+ ft) thick	Moderate to high	Poorly welded, friable and weak for road & buildings foundations, trails and camp sites; variable permeability may allow waste facility development.	Degree of welding highly heterogeneous; erosion, slides and slumping probable.	None	None documented	None	Volcanic landscaping rock; Ash flow tuffs; breccia locally present	Vugs and vesicles, if large, enough can provide habitat	Suitable for most recreation	27-26 Ma tuff layer
Tertiary (U. Eocene - Oligocene)	Brian Head Formation (Tbh)	Three poorly exposed units: 1) lower soft, reddish-brown, pink, & reddish-orange, non-tuffaceous sandstone & conglomerate with some siltstone, claystone, & micritic limestone; 2) gray, greenish-gray, yellowish-gray, bioturbated beds of volcaniclastic clayey sandstone, conglomeratic sandstone, claystone, micritic limestone, & air fall tuff; 3) upper heterogeneous unit of volcanic mudflow breccia, immature volcanic sandstone and conglomerate, mafic lava flows, and ash-flow tuff; total thickness: 213 m (700 ft).	Moderate	Variable in rock type, degree of consolidation and stability; careful mapping and surveying recommended before development; some swelling clay.	High potential for rockfalls and landslides especially when exposed on a slope or undercut by erosion of underlying layers	Vertebrates Plants	Chert may have provided tool material in this unit	None	Flagstone, building material, chalcedony root casts	None documented	Suitable for most recreation	Possibly a type section in monument
Tertiary (Eocene)	Claron Formation, White Member (Tcw)	Lake & river sediments; cliff of white & light-orange, micritic limestone; yellowish-gray to light-brown, interbedded mudstone and fine- to medium-grained sandstone; cliff of white, light yellowish-gray, and light-orange, micritic limestone; forms impressive, west-facing scarp marking the rim of the central Markagunt Plateau; about 110 m (360 ft) thick.	Moderate	Hoodoos and other erosional and karst features are abundant in this unit making development a poor candidate for development.	Slumping, sliding and rockfall potential when highly eroded or undercut from lower units on a slope face	Locally abundant palynomorphs, insects and assorted gastropods	Erosional formations often had spiritual significance to ancient Native American tribes	High	Limestone; Some sparry calcite and chalcedony	Hoodoos and other erosional features create cavities and cliffs for habitat	Erodibility and delicate nature of hoodoos discourages recreational use	Type section potential
Tertiary (Paleocene - Eocene)	Claron Formation, Red Member (Tcr)	Resistant pink, red, & reddish-orange, argillaceous, sandy micritic limestone; resistant reddish-tan & pink cross-bedded sandstone; soft, red and pink silty mudstone with minor lenticular, gray, pink, reddish-tan, resistant conglomerate and conglomeratic sandstone; 65-foot limestone at base. Thin-bedded limestone, cross-bedded sandstone, and lenticular conglomerate beds are more resistant than soft mudstone beds; veinlets of sparry calcite that represent algal filaments branch through the limestone also containing vertical burrow fillings and stylolites. Shallow caves and local springs found in 65-foot limestone bed at base; approximately 296 m (700 ft) thick.	Moderate	Hoodoos and other erosional and karst features abundant; a poor candidate for development.	Severe erosion hazards; landslide potential rockfall potential, especially where exposed on steep slopes	Pelecypods, gastropods and other trace fossils abundant.	Hoodoos and other erosional formations had significant spiritual significance to local ancient Native American peoples	High	Limestone; Caliche beds	Hoodoos and other erosional features create cavities and cliffs for habitat	Erodibility and delicate nature of hoodoos discourages recreational use	Type section potential

Age	Unit Name (Symbol)	Features and Description	Erosion Resistance	Suitability for Development	Hazards	Potential Paleontologic Resources	Potential Cultural Resources	Potential for Karst	Mineral Resources & Specimens	Habitat	Recreation Potential	Global Significance
Upper Cretaceous–Tertiary (Paleocene)	Grand Castle and Wahweap Sandstones (TKgw)	Mostly sandstone in upper part of Wahweap; rest of formation poorly exposed, interbedded soft, mostly brownish- gray, olive- brown, and reddish-brown mudstone with minor sandstone and siltstone. Thin- bedded siltstone and fine- grained sandstone is gray, black, and grayish- orange; sandstone locally cross-bedded (Hatfield et al., 2000). Carbonized fossil wood, leaf impressions, and spherical calcareous, limonitic concretions present; lower part of the unit is a poorly exposed friable, cross- bedded sandstone; light gray to light yellowish- gray and locally interbedded with underlying Wahweap Sandstone; upper part is a ledge of fine- to coarse- grained, cross- bedded, argillaceous, cherty sandstone and small-pebble mudstone conglomerate. The angular, poorly to moderately sorted sandstone is yellowish- brown, orange-gray, and white "salt- and- pepper"; may correlate with Grand Castle Fm; combined thickness averages 305 m (1000+ ft).	Moderate to high	Suitable for most forms of development unless highly fractured or undercut on a slope; variable in rock type; careful mapping and development needed; mud- rich units & poorly consolidated units will compromise stability of structures and roads.	High variability of rock types may create rockfalls when a resistant unit overlies a less resistant unit; sliding potential in mud- rich or poorly consolidated layers.	Leaf impressions, some fossil wood, pelecypods and other assorted vertebrate fossils found regionally	Possible tool material	Low; little carbonate present	Limonite, pyrite concretions, flagstone material	Vugs in cliffs may provide nesting habitat	Suitable for most forms of recreation unless poorly cemented on slopes	Controversy over origin and designation of unit
Upper Cretaceous	Straight Cliffs Formation, upper part (Kscu)	Soft, light- gray, yellowish- gray, light yellowish- brown, reddish- brown, & brownish- gray mudstone with thin beds of lenticular, fine- to medium- grained sandstone; sandstone thickens to west where lower unit forms gray cliffs of marine sandstone interbedded with thin beds of fossiliferous oyster- bearing limestone and coal; oyster- bearing limestone and coal to the west of CEBR; about 366 m (1200 ft) thick.	High	Suitable for most forms of development unless highly fractured or undercut on a slope exposure.	Rockfall potential when exposed on a cliff face	Some fossil wood, oysters, clams and assorted gastropods	Provided building material for ancient Native Americans; petroglyphs present at some locales	Low; little carbonate present	Coal beds	Vugs in cliffs may provide nesting habitat	Suitable for most forms of recreation unless on slope forming uppermost beds; climbing discouraged in upper parts of unit	Correlated with Iron Springs Formation of the Basin and Range

Geologic History

This section highlights the map units (i.e., rocks and unconsolidated deposits) that occur in Cedar Breaks National Monument and puts them in a geologic context in terms of the environment in which they were deposited and the timing of geologic events that created the present landscape.

The geologic story of Cedar Breaks National Monument begins in the Late Cretaceous (figure 5). Dinosaurs roamed southwestern and western Utah, feeding on lush vegetation while other vertebrates and abundant invertebrate inhabited the ocean and near shore environments to the east of Cedar Breaks. As the Sevier Orogeny advanced from the west, sedimentary rocks that had formed in shallow, offshore marine environments were folded and uplifted into mountain ranges.

In complement to the uplifting mountains, the Western Interior Basin, a shallow north- south trending basin, formed east of the thrust belt. While the mountains rose in the west and the Western Interior Basin expanded, the Gulf of Mexico separating North and South America rift open in the south, and marine water began flowing northward into the basin. At the same time, marine water began to advance onto the continent from the Arctic region. As the shallow seas advanced onto the continent, currents redistributed sediment deposited by river systems in much the same way sediments are redistributed along the shorelines of North America today. As more sediment was shed from the continent and deposited into the basin, the weight of the sediment caused the basin to subside.

The seas advanced and retreated many times during the Cretaceous until the most extensive interior seaway ever recorded drowned much of western North America (figure 6). The Western Interior Seaway filled an elongate basin that extended from today's Gulf of Mexico to the Arctic Ocean, a distance of about 4827 km (3,000 mi) (Kauffman 1977).

In the Cretaceous the western margin of the seaway coincided with the active Sevier orogenic belt, but the eastern margin was part of the low- lying, stable platform ramp in what today coincides with Nebraska and Kansas. Consequently, sedimentation into the basin from the rising mountains on the western margin was rapid compared to the slow sedimentation into the basin from the craton on the eastern margin. Rapid sedimentation led to further sediment loading and downwarping along the western margin.

By the Late Cretaceous, the present Four- Corners area had migrated northward into a subtropical climatic zone. Although the seaway was not physically restricted at either end, water circulation appears to have been periodically disrupted. A variety of depositional environments existed throughout the basin as sea level rose and fell. These included brackish estuaries, deltas, beaches, deep water, coal swamps, and fluvial systems.

Over time, changes in depositional environment with changing sea level were recorded in the vertical section of rocks and fossils.

The Straight Cliffs Formation and Grand Castle-Wahweap Sandstone record a gradual change from nearshore, mostly shallow marine environments in the Straight Cliffs to fluvial (river) and lake deposition in the Grand Castle and Wahweap Sandstone. In effect, these Late Cretaceous to early Tertiary rocks record the Sevier orogenic deformation and its evolution into Laramide-style deformation (Goldstrand 1990). For about 35 million years during the Laramide Orogeny, from roughly 70 Ma to 35 Ma, the collision of the tectonic plates transformed the extensive basin of the Cretaceous Interior Seaway into smaller, internally drained, non-marine, intermontane basins (figure 7) (Goldstrand 1990; Ott 1999; Graham et al. 2002). This style, contrasting with earlier Sevier deformation, involved thick, basement-cored uplifts along thrust faults, and extensive folding.

According to Gilbert (1877):

> "It seems as though the crust of the earth had been divided into great blocks, each many miles in extent, which were moved from their original positions in various ways. Some were carried up and others down, and the majority were left higher at one margin than at the other. But although they moved independently, they were not cleft asunder. The strata remained continuous, and were flexed instead of faulted at the margins of the blocks."

The Claron Formation includes fluvial, deltaic, and lacustrine sediments, deposited after the Sevier Orogeny ended. These sediments record deposition in well-aerated lakes and streams in a large, stable intermontane basin bounded by the basement- cored uplifts produced during the Laramide Orogeny (figure 8) (Goldstrand 1990; Ott 1999; Hatfield et al. 2000).

The lower red member of the Claron Formation was deposited in a shallow, low- energy, low gradient lake margin, resulting in the slow alteration and pedogenesis (extreme bioturbation) of the primary sediments. The upper white member signals the reestablishments of continuous lacustrine sedimentation punctuated by rare pedogenic (soil forming) events (Ott 1999). The upper layers, which might bear record of the desiccation of the lacustrine environment, have been eroded from the Cedar Breaks area.

The angle at which the Pacific lithospheric plate was being subducted beneath the North American plate changed in the Eocene and cut off the Laramide Orogeny. The shallow basins continued to be filled with lake and stream deposits that eventually became the Brian Head Formation (Eocene and Oligocene). The lower part of the Brian Head Formation reflects a continuation of the relatively passive environmental setting that began in the Late Cretaceous. Dinosaurs were absent and streams that traversed the hummocky topography carried silt and mud that slowly settled into the remaining lakes.

The tuffaceous sediments in the middle parts of the Brian Head Formation mark the beginning of extensive volcanic eruptions to the west and north that impacted not only Utah but also the entire margin of western North America. About 32 Ma (lower Oligocene), clustered volcanoes explosively erupted in stratovolcanoes that became the Marysvale volcanic field. The southern margin of this volcanic field lies just north of the monument.

Explosive andesitic volcanism dominated the area to the west during Oligocene and early Miocene time and probably inundated both the Cedar Breaks and Zion regions with hundreds of feet of volcanic ash (figure 9) (Biek et al. 2000; Hatfield et al. 2000). Like the ash deposits from Mt. St. Helens, the Tertiary volcanic ash erupted as a hot mixture of volcanic gases and tephra forming the ash- flow tuffs of the Isom Formation (27 Ma; Oligocene) and the Leach Canyon Formation (24 Ma; Miocene).

Coincident with basaltic volcanism, the north- striking faults of the ancestral Hurricane fault zone ruptured the surface. North of Cedar Breaks, deep grabens developed by west- northwest striking faults active about 26 Ma. These grabens filled with eolian sand, volcanic ash, and mafic lava flows seen today as the Bear Valley Formation (not exposed in the monument) (Hatfield et al. 2000). Volcanic mudflows (lahars) surged down the flanks of the denuded volcanoes of the Marysvale volcanic field and buried the Bear Valley Formation. These became the volcanic breccias of the Mount Dutton Formation (not exposed in the monument).

During the Lower Miocene (22 to 20 Ma), the Markagunt Megabreccia moved southward into the Cedar Breaks area. This movement was triggered either by earthquakes causing movement on giant gravity- slide sheets or by compressive forces that caused shallow thrust sheets in and north of the monument to rupture the surface. The megabreccia slid along subhorizontal shear planes in incompetent rock units such as the Brian Head Formation.

The Basin and Range extensional tectonic episode began in southwestern Utah about 20 Ma although most basin and range faulting began about 10 Ma (Hatfield et al. 2000). The major result of this extension was creation of the Basin and Range Province to the west. In this period of extension, the Hurricane Fault Zone underwent its

most recent episode of faulting and the High Plateaus were blocked out. Extensional tectonics have continued to the present.

Uplift of the Markagunt Plateau was accompanied by extensive erosion. Rocks were loosened by physical weathering such as frost action and root growth and by chemical weathering such as the dissolution of the calcium carbonate cement that binds the particles together to form sedimentary rock. Once loosened, the particles cascade downslope by the force of gravity or are removed by runoff from rain or melting snow. Rivers also cut into the cliffs by headward erosion. Headward erosion carves shallow, elongate indentations or amphitheaters into the edge of a plateau. Not all rocks erode in the same manner. Some are more resistant than others. This selective erosion of less resistant rock is called differential erosion.

At Cedar Breaks National Monument, the erosion of the fault scarp bordering the Markagunt Plateau has caused the western margin to retreat several miles eastward. During the Pleistocene, the highest parts of the plateau in Cedar Breaks were scoured and scraped by glaciers. Physical and chemical weathering including mass wasting by landslides, rock falls and soil creep continue to erode the plateau's rim and push it farther eastward. The topography we see now at Cedar Breaks will slowly disappear as the landscape continues to evolve.

The Quaternary Period is subdivided into two epochs: 1) Pleistocene, which ranges from about 1.6 Ma to 10,000 years before present (B.P.), and 2) Holocene Epoch that extends from 10,000 years B.P. to the present. The Pleistocene Epoch is known as the Ice Age and is marked by multiple episodes of continental and alpine glaciation. Continental glaciers, thousands of feet thick, advanced and retreated over approximately 100,000- year cycles.

Huge volumes of water were stored in the glaciers during glacial periods so that sea level dropped as much as 91 m (300 ft) (Fillmore 2000). The carving of a rugged mountain landscape by streams, frost action, and glaciers has been the principal geologic activity in this region from late Tertiary time to the present.

The Holocene is the Age of Humans and human impact on the global ecosystem is complex. With the retreat of the glaciers and the end of widespread glaciation about 12,000 years ago, the climate continued to warm and global sea level rose. In some local areas (e.g., the coast of Maine), however, relative sea level lowered as the land rebounded from the weight of the glaciers. Local tectonism, sediment input, global warming, and global cooling are some of the factors affecting global sea level The relative importance of these factors, and the impacts that humans have on them, continue to be debated today (Graham et al. 2002).

Geologically, the High Plateaus area has not changed much during the Holocene. The area has been subjected to some extension and uplift associated with the Rio Grande Rift, and streams have carved new landscapes since the end of the Ice Age. However this is geologically a very brief period of time. Figure 10 summarizes the geologic history from the Proterozoic to the present at Cedar Breaks.

The following references provide additional information regarding geologic principles, the geology of Cedar Breaks National Monument, and background information on the monument.

- Plummer, C. C., McGeary, D., and Carlson, D. H., 1996, Physical Geology: McGraw- Hill, 577 p.

- Chernicoff, S. and Venkatakrishnan, R., 1995, Geology, Worth Publishers, 593 p.

- Tarbuck, E. J., Lutgens, F. K., and Dennis, T., 2001, Earth: An Introduction to Physical Geology: Prentice-Hall, 7th edition, 688 p.

- Hatfield, S.C., Rowley, P.D., Sable, E.G., Maxwell, D.J., Cox, B.V., McKell, M.D., Kiel, D.E., 2000, Geology of Cedar Breaks National Monument, in D.A. Sprinkel, T.C. Chidsey, Jr., and P.B. Anderson, eds., Geology of Utah's Parks and Monuments: Utah Geological Association, Publication 28, p. 139- 154.

- Kiver, E.P. and Harris, D.V., 1999, Geology of U.S. Parklands: John Wiley & Sons, Inc., New York, 5th Edition, p. 522- 530.

Eon	Era	Period	Epoch	Ma	Life Forms	N. American Tectonics
Phanerozoic (Phaneros = "evident"; zoic = "life")	Cenozoic	Quaternary	Recent, or Holocene		Age of Mammals — Modern man	Cascade volcanoes
				0.8	Extinction of large mammals and birds	
			Pleistocene			Worldwide glaciation
				1.8		
			Pliocene		Large carnivores	Uplift of Sierra Nevada
		Tertiary		5.3	Whales and apes	Linking of N. & S. America
			Miocene	23.8		
			Oligocene			Basin-and-Range Extension
				33.7		
			Eocene	55.5	Early primates	Laramide orogeny ends (West)
			Paleocene			
				— 65 —		
	Mesozoic	Cretaceous			Age of Dinosaurs — **Mass extinctions**	Laramide orogeny (West)
					Placental mammals	Sevier orogeny (West)
				145	Early flowering plants	Nevadan orogeny (West)
		Jurassic			First mammals	Elko orogeny (West)
				213	Flying reptiles	Breakup of Pangea begins
		Triassic			First dinosaurs	Sonoma orogeny (West)
				— 248 —		
	Paleozoic	Permian			Age of Amphibians — **Mass extinctions**	Super continent Pangea intact
					Coal-forming forests diminish	Ouachita orogeny (South) Alleghenian (Appalachian) orogeny (East)
				286		Ancestral Rocky Mts. (West)
		Pennsylvanian			Coal-forming swamps Sharks abundant	
				325	Variety of insects	
		Mississippian			First amphibians	
				360	First reptiles	Antler orogeny (West)
		Devonian			Fishes — **Mass extinctions** First forests (evergreens)	Acadian orogeny (East-NE)
				410		
		Silurian			First land plants	
				440	**Mass extinctions** First primitive fish	
		Ordovician			Marine Invertebrates — Trilobite maximum Rise of corals	Taconic orogeny (NE)
				505		
		Cambrian				Avalonian orogeny (NE)
					Early shelled organisms	Extensive oceans cover most of N. America
				— 544 —		
Proterozoic ("Early life")		Precambrian			1st multicelled organisms	Formation of early supercontinent
						First iron deposits
					Jellyfish fossil (670Ma)	Abundant carbonate rocks
Archean ("Ancient")				2500		
					Early bacteria & algae	
				~3800		Oldest known Earth rocks (~3.93 billion years ago)
Hadean ("Beneath the Earth")					Origin of life?	Oldest moon rocks (4-4.6 billion years ago)
						Earth's crust being formed
				— 4600 —	Formation of the Earth	

Figure 5. Geologic time scale; adapted from the U.S. Geological Survey. Red lines indicate major unconformities between eras. Included are major events in life history and tectonic events occurring on the North American continent. Absolute ages shown are in millions of years.

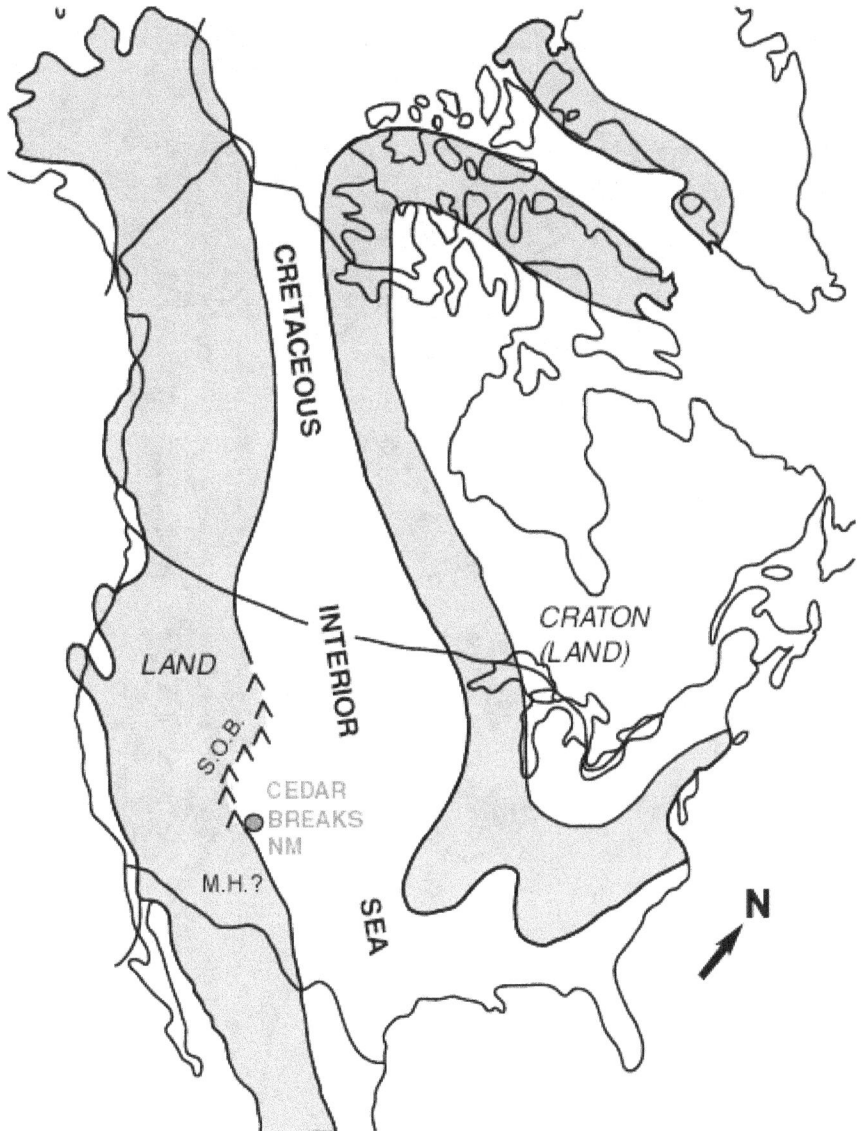

Figure 6. Location of the Cretaceous Period, Western Interior Seaway. Shaded areas indicate land above sea level. Shoreline migrated east and west periodically through time. North indicates the Cretaceous north. Modified from Rice and Shurr (1983).

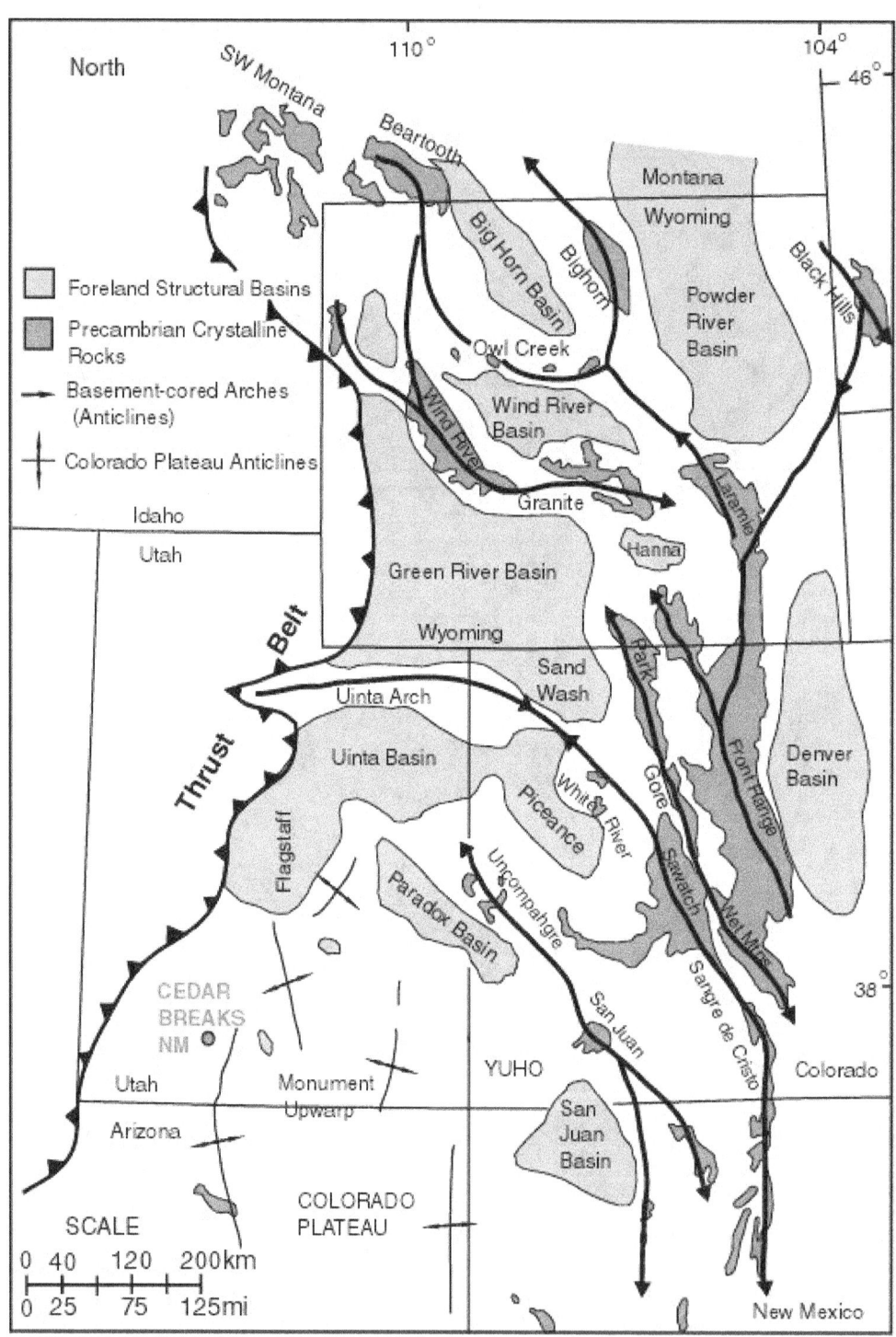

Figure 7. Location of Cedar Breaks National Monument on a tectonic map showing Laramide-age structures on the Colorado Plateau. The map illustrates the anastamosing nature of the basement-cored arches (regional-scale anticlines) and the spatial relationships with the adjacent thrust belt, Colorado Plateau, and North American craton. The 'Thrust Belt' marks the eastern extent of the Sevier Orogeny. From Gregson and Chure, 2000.

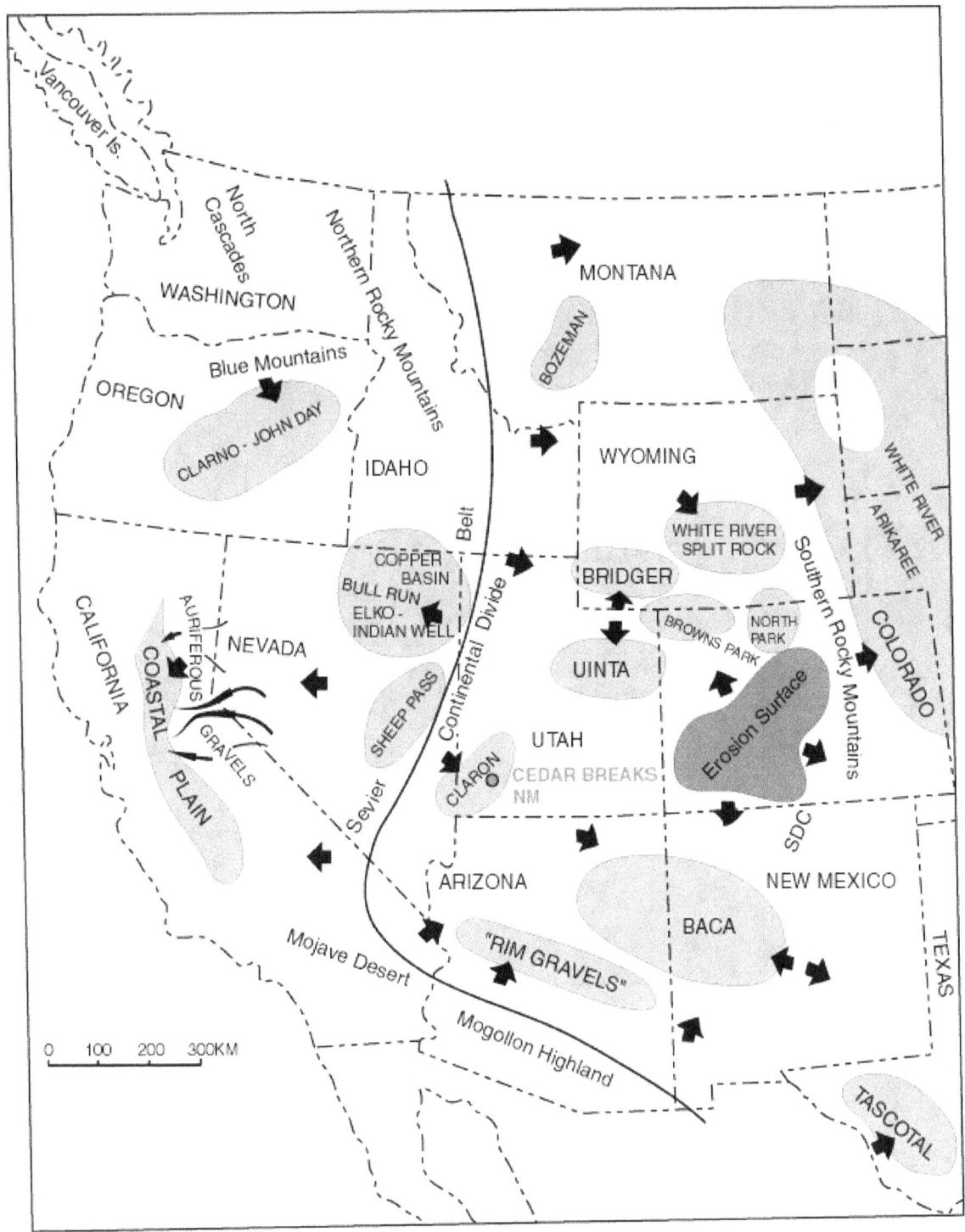

Figure 8. Early post-Laramide map showing the probable location of the continental divide, major depositional basins, erosional features, and stream systems in the western U.S. Light gray areas denote basins (note Claron Basin), dark gray areas indicate highlands and arrows indicate probable directions of sediment transport into the basins and away from the continental divide. SDC, Sangre de Cristo Mountains; SJ, San Juan Mountains. Modified from Christiansen and others, 1992.

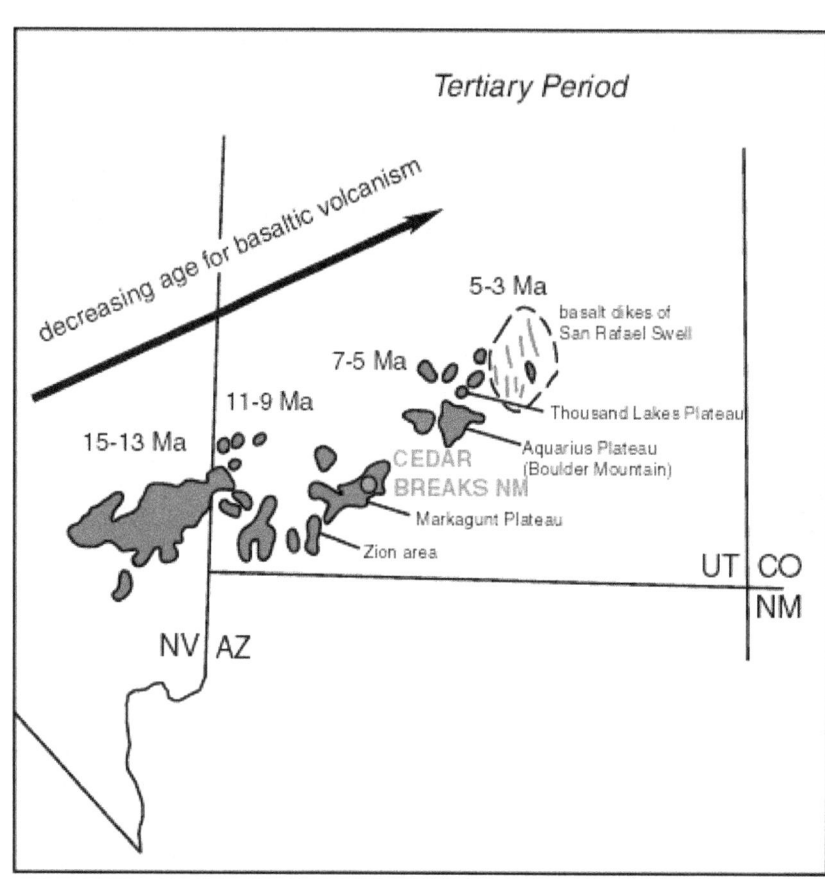

Figure 9. Tertiary (primarily Miocene) volcanic centers in southern Utah and Nevada. The ages of the basalt systematically decrease from west to east, suggesting the presence of a fixed hot spot in the mantle. Modified from Fillmore, 2000, and Nelson and Tingey, 1997.

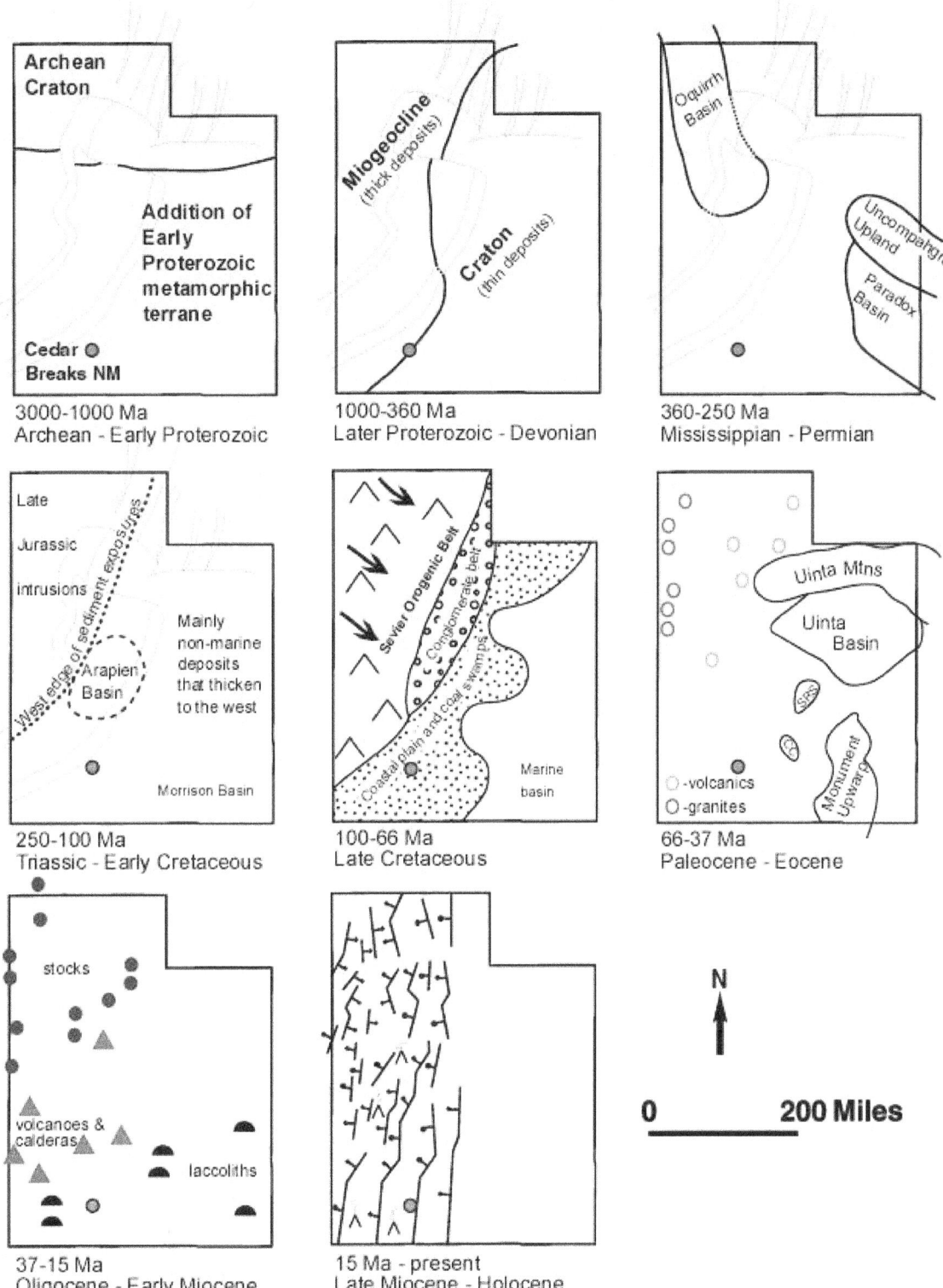

Figure 10. Generalized graphic overview of geologic evolution of Utah from the Archean Eon to the Holocene Epoch (adapted from Hintze 1988).

References

This section provides a listing of references cited in this report. It also contains general references that may be of use to resource managers. A more complete geologic bibliography is available and can be obtained through the NPS Geologic Resources Division.

Baars, D.L., Bartleson, B.L., Chapin, C.E., Curtis, B.F., De Voto R.H., Everett, J.R., Johnson, R.C., Molenaar, D.M., Peterson, F., Schenk, C.J., Love, J.D., Merin, I;.S., Rose, P.R., Ryder, R.T., Waechter, N.B., and Woodward, L.A., 1988, Basins of the Rocky Mountain region, in L.L. Sloss, ed., Sedimentary Cover – North American Craton: U.S.: Geological Society of America, The Geology of North America, Volume D- 2, p. 109-220.

Biek, R.F., Willis, G.C., Hylland, M.D., and Doelling, H.H., 2000, Geology of Zion National Park, Utah, in D.A. Sprinkel, T.C. Chidsey, Jr., and P.B. Anderson, eds., Geology of Utah's Parks and Monuments: Utah Geological Association Publication 28, p. 107- 138.

Bown, T. M., S. T. Hasiotis, J. F. Genise, F. Maldonado, and E. M. Brouwers. 1997. Trace fossils of Hymenoptera and other insects, and paleoenvironments of the Claron Formation (Paleocene and Eocene), southwestern Utah. Pages 41-58 in F. Maldonado and L. D. Nealey (editors). Geologic studies in the Basin and Range- Colorado Plateau transition in southeastern Nevada, southeastern Utah, and northwestern Arizona, 1995. U.S. Geological Survey Bulletin 2153.

Brox, G.S., 1961, The geology (Wasatch Formation, Eocene) and erosional development of northern Bryce Canyon National Park, (Garfield County, Utah). Master's thesis, University of Utah, Salt Lake City, UT, 70 pp.

Chenoweth, W. L., 1996, The Uranium industry in the Paradox Basin, in A.C. Huffman, Jr., W.R. Lund, and L.H. Godwin, eds., Geology and Resources of the Paradox Basin: Utah Geological Association Guidebook 25, 1996 Field Symposium, p. 95- 108.

De Courten, F., 1994, Shadows of time – the geology of Bryce Canyon National Park. Bryce Canyon Natural History Association, Bryce Canyon, Utah, 128 pp.

Dutton, C.E., 1880, Report on the geology of the High Plateaus of Utah. U.S. Geographic and Geological Survey of the Rocky Mountain region (Powell), 307 pp.

Eaton, J. G., S. Diem, J. D. Archibald, C. Schierup, and H. Munk. 1999a. Vertebrate paleontology of the Upper Cretaceous roks of the Markagunt Plateau, southwestern Utah. Pages 323- 334 in Gillette, D. D. (editor). Vertebrate Paleontology in Utah. Utah Geological Survey Miscellaneous Publication 99- 1.

Eaton, J. G., J. H. Hutchison, P. A. Holroyd, W. W. Korth, and P. M. Goldstrand. 1999b. Vertebrates of the Turtle Basin local fauna, Middle Eocene, Sevier Plateau, South- Central Utah. Pages 463- 468 in Gillette, D. D. (editor). Vertebrate Paleontology in Utah. Utah Geological Survey Miscellaneous Publication 99- 1.

Fillmore, R., 2000, The Geology of the Parks, Monuments and Wildlands of Southern Utah: The University of Utah Press, 268 p.

Goldstrand, P.M., 1990, Stratigraphy and paleogeography of Late Cretaceous and Paleogene rocks of southwest Utah: Utah Geological and Mineral Survey Miscellaneous Publication 90- 2, 58 p.

Goldstrand, P.M., 1994, Tectonic development of Upper Cretaceous to Eocene strata of southwestern Utah: Geological Society of American Bulletin, v. 106, no. 1, p. 145- 154.

Graham, J. P., Thornberry, T. L., and O'Meara, S. A., 2002, Geologic Resources Inventory for Capitol Reef National Park: Inventory and Monitoring Program, National Park Service, Fort Collins, CO., 328 p.

Gregory, H.E., 1950, Geology and Geography of the Zion Park Region Utah and Arizona: U.S.G.S. Professional Paper 220, 200 p.

Gregory, H.E., 1951, The geology and geography of the Paunsaugunt region, Utah: USGS Professional Paper 226, 116 p.

Gregory, H.E., Moore, R.C., 1931, The Kaiparowits region, a geographical and geologic reconnaissance of parts of Utah and Arizona. U.S. Geological Survey Professional Paper 164, 161 pp.

Hatfield, S. C., P. D. Rowley, E. G. Sable, D. J. Maxwell, B. V. Cox, M. D. McKell, and D. E. Kiel. 2000a. Geology of Cedar Breaks National Monument, Utah. in Sprinkel, D. A., T. C. Chidsey, Jr. and P. B. Anderson (editors). Geology of Utah's Parks and Monuments. Utah Geological Association Publication 28.

Hatfield, S. C., P. D. Rowley, E. G. Sable, D. J. Maxwell, B. V. Cox, M. D. McKell, and D. E. Kiel. 2000b. Geologic Road Log of Cedar Breaks National Monument, Utah. in Anderson, P. B. and D. A. Sprinkel, (editors). Geologic Road, Trail, and Lake Guides to Utah's Parks and Monuments. Utah Geological Association Publication 29.

Hintze, L.F., 1988, 1993, Geologic history of Utah: Brigham Young University Studies Special Publication 7, 202 p.

Kauffman, E. G., 1977, Geological and biological overview: Western Interior Cretaceous Basin: Mountain Geologist, v. 14, p. 75- 99.

Kelley, V.C., 1955, Monoclines of the Colorado Plateau. Geological Society of America Bulletin, vol. 66, pp. 789- 804.

Kelley, V.C., Clinton, N.J., 1960, Fracture systems and tectonic elements of the Colorado Plateau. University of New Mexico Publications in Geology, no. 6, 104 pp.

Kiver, E.P. and Harris, D.V., 1999, Geology of U.S. Parklands: John Wiley & Sons, Inc., 5th edition, p. 455- 466.

Lindquist, R.C., 1980, Slope processes and forms at Bryce Canyon National Park. Dissertation, University of Utah, Salt Lake City, UT, 134 pp.

Nelson, S.T., and Tingey, D.G., 1997, Time- transgressive and extension- related basaltic volcanism in southwest Utah and vicinity: Geological Society of America Bulletin 109, p. 1249- 1265.

Nuccio, V. F. and Condon, S. M., 1996, Burial and thermal history of the Paradox Basin, Utah and Colorado, and petroleum potential of the Middle Pennsylvanian Paradox Formation, in A.C. Huffman, Jr., W.R. Lund, and L.H. Godwin, eds., Geology and Resources of the Paradox Basin: Utah Geological Association Guidebook 25, 1996 Field Symposium, p. 57- 76.

Ott, A.L., 1999, Detailed stratigraphy and stable isotope analysis of the Claron Formation, Bryce Canyon National Park, southwestern Utah. Master's Thesis, Washington State University, Pullman, WA.

Rice, D. D. and Shurr, G. W., 1983, Patterns of sedimentation and paleogeography across the Western Interior Seaway during time of deposition of Upper Cretaceous Eagle Sandstone and equivalent rocks, northern Great Plains, in M. W. Reynolds and E. D. Dolly, eds., Mesozoic Paleogeography of the West- Central United States: Rocky Mountain Section, SEPM (Society for Sedimentary Geology), p. 337- 358.

Santucci, Vincent L., Kenworthy, Jason, and Kerbo, Ron, 2001, An inventory of paleontological resources associated with National Park Service Caves, Geologic Resources Division Technical Report 01/02, p.10.

State of Utah, 2004, Coal Resources. http://www.planning.utah.gov/CRMPCoalResources. htm

Swan, F.H., III, Schwartz, D.P., Cluff, L.S., 1980, Recurrence of moderate to large magnitude earthquakes produced by surface faulting on the Wasatch fault zone, Utah. Bulletin Seismological Society of America, vol. 70, pp. 1431- 1432.

Appendix A: Geologic Map Graphic

The following page provides a preview or "snapshot" of the geologic map for Cedar Breaks National Monument. For a poster size PDF of this map or for digital geologic map data, please see the included CD or visit the GRE publications webpage: http://www2.nature.nps.gov/geology/inventory/gre_publications.cfm

Geologic Map of Cedar Breaks NM

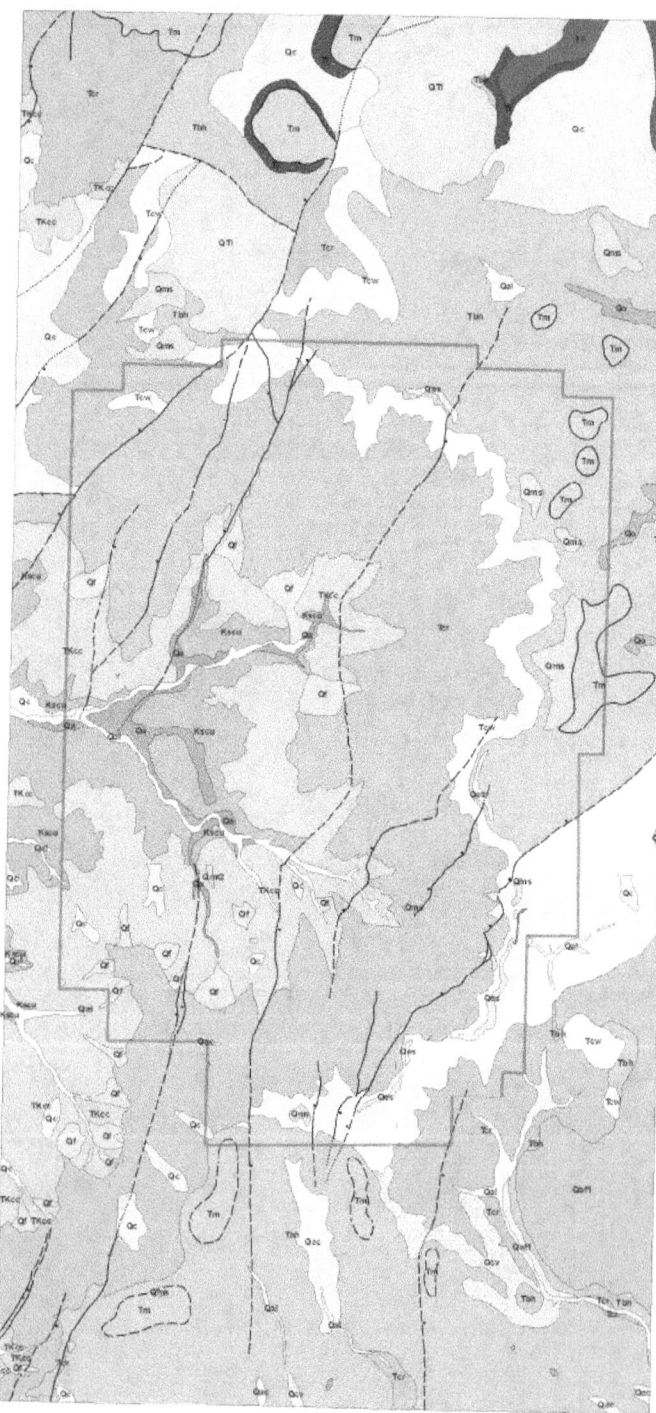

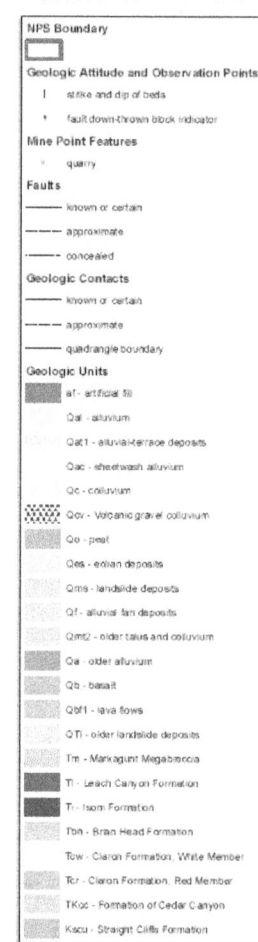

NPS Boundary

Geologic Attitude and Observation Points

| strike and dip of beds

• fault down-thrown block indicator

Mine Point Features

• quarry

Faults

—— known or certain

—— — approximate

– – – concealed

Geologic Contacts

—— known or certain

—— — approximate

– – – quadrangle boundary

Geologic Units

- af - artificial fill
- Qal - alluvium
- Qat1 - alluvial-terrace deposits
- Qac - sheetwash alluvium
- Qc - colluvium
- Qcv - Volcanic gravel colluvium
- Qo - peat
- Qes - eolian deposits
- Qms - landslide deposits
- Qf - alluvial fan deposits
- Qmt2 - older talus and colluvium
- Qa - older alluvium
- Qb - basalt
- Qbf1 - lava flows
- QTl - older landslide deposits
- Tm - Markagunt Megabreccia
- Tl - Leach Canyon Formation
- Ti - Isom Formation
- Tbh - Bran Head Formation
- Tcw - Claron Formation, White Member
- Tcr - Claron Formation, Red Member
- TKcc - Formation of Cedar Canyon
- Kscu - Straight Cliffs Formation

The original maps digitized by NPS staff to create this product were:

Moore, David W., Nealey, L. David, 1993, Preliminary Geologic Map of Navajo Lake Quadrangle, Kane and Iron Counties, Utah: U.S. Geological Survey, Open File Report, OF 93-190, scale 1:24,000

Hatfield, Stanley C., Rowley, Peter D., Sable, Edward G., Maxwell, David J., Cox, Bryant V., McKell, Matthew D., Kiel, David E., 2000, Geology of Cedar Breaks National Monument, Utah, in Sprinkel, D.A., Chidsey, T.C. Jr., Anderson, P.B. eds Geology of Utah's Parks and Monuments, Utah Geological Association Publication 28, 2000 UGA

Moore, D.W., Nealey, L.D., Rowley, P.D., Hatfield, S.C., Maxwell, D.J., Mitchell, E., 2002, Geologic Map of Navajo Lake Quadrangle, Kane and Iron Counties, Utah: U.S. Geological Survey MOORE 2002 scale 1:24,000

Digital geologic data and cross sections for Cedar Breaks National Monument, and all other digital geologic data prepared as part of the Geologic Resources Divisions Geologic Resource Evaluation program, are available online:
http://www2.nature.nps.gov/geology/inventory/gre_publications.cfm

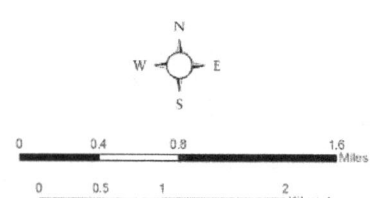

| 0 | 0.4 | 0.8 | 1.6 |
Miles

| 0 | 0.5 | 1 | 2 |
Kilometers

Appendix B: Scoping Summary

The following excerpts are from the GRE scoping summary for Cedar Breaks National Monument. The scoping meeting occurred on July 15- 16, 1999; therefore, the contact information and Web addresses referred to herein may be outdated. Please contact the Geologic Resources Division for current information.

Executive Summary

An evaluation workshop was held at Cedar Breaks National Monument on July 15- 16, 1999 to view and discuss the park's geologic resources, to address the status of geologic mapping by both the Utah Geological Survey (UGS) and the United States Geological Survey (USGS) for compiling both paper and digital maps, and to assess resource management issues and needs. Cooperators from the NPS Geologic Resources Division (GRD), Natural Resources Information Division (NRID), Cedar Breaks NM, UGS, USGS, Southern Utah University, Stockton College, USFS and Utah Bureau of Land Management (BLM) were present for the two- day workshop.

Day one involved a field trip co- led by SUU geology professor Stan Hatfield and USGS geologist Pete Rowley.

Day two involved a scoping session to present overviews of the NPS Inventory and Monitoring (I&M) program, the Geologic Resources Division, and the ongoing Geologic Resource Evaluation (GRE) for Colorado and Utah. Round table discussions involving geologic issues for Cedar Breaks NM included interpretation, the UGA Millennium 2000 guidebook featuring the geology of Utah's National and State parks, the status of cooperative geologic mapping efforts, sources of available data, geologic hazards, potential future research topics, and action items generated from this meeting. Brief summaries of each follow.

Overview of Geologic Resource Evaluation

After introductions by the participants, Steve Fryer (NPS- NRID) presented an overview of the NPS I&M Program, the status of the natural resource inventories, and the geological resources inventory.

He also presented a demonstration of some of the main features of the digital geologic map for the Black Canyon of the Gunnison NM and Curecanti NRA areas in Colorado. This has become the prototype for the NPS digital geologic map model as it ideally reproduces all aspects of a paper map (i.e. it incorporates the map notes, cross- sections, legend etc.) with the added benefit of being a GIS component.

It is displayed in ESRI ArcView shape files and features a built- in help file system to identify the map units. It can also display scanned JPG or GIF images of the geologic cross sections supplied with the map. The cross section lines (ex. A- A') are subsequently digitized as a shape file and are hyperlinked to the scanned images

For a recap on this process, go to: http://www.nature.nps.gov/grd/geology/gri/blca_cure/ and view the various files in the directory.

The geologists at the workshop familiar with GIS methods were quite impressed with this method of displaying geologic maps digitally; Joe Gregson is to be commended for his accomplishments.

Bruce Heise (NPS- GRD) followed with an overview of the Geologic Resources Division and the Geologic Resource Evaluation program.

The GRE also aims to help promote geologic resource interpretation within the parks and GRD has staff and technology to assist in preparation of useful materials including developing site bulletins and resource management proposal (RMP) statements appropriate to promoting geology. Jim Wood (GRD) and Melanie Moreno (USGS- Menlo Park, CA) have worked with several other NPS units in developing web- based geology interpretation themes, and should be considered as a source of assistance should the park desire.

The UGS has the Geologic Extension Services available for help to the NPS for creating interpretive brochures and for seasonal employee training. The UGS also has programs for applied geology (hazards), economic geology, archeology and paleontology. Pete Rowley and Stan Hatfield have generously offered their services and are also available locally for any assistance the park may need regarding geologic issues and interpretation.

UGA Guidebook on Utah's National and State Park Areas

Grant Willis of the UGA announced that a guidebook treating the geology of 27 of Utah's national and state parks and monuments would be compiled for publication in September 2000. This compilation will be a snapshot into the geology of each park and covers most facets of what the GRE is trying to develop for each park for a final report (i.e. cross sections, simplified geologic map, general discussions of rocks, structure, unique aspects of park geology, classic viewing localities). The only NPS unit in Utah that will not be treated will be Golden Spike National Historic Site.

Funding for this publication is coming jointly from the UGA, NPS, BLM, USFS and Utah state parks; it is hoped that the publication will be sold for under $30.

Each author will be encouraged to get with NPS staff interpreters to develop a product that aims at a wide audience (the common visitor, the technical audience and the teaching community). Cedar Breaks NM authors will be our field trip leaders (Stan Hatfield, who has also tried to enlist the services of Pete Rowley into the project).

Park authors are strongly encouraged to get with NPS staff to make sure that any trail logs do follow maintained trails and do not take visitors into unauthorized areas, or places where resources are fragile and would be disturbed by increased visitation (i.e. areas with cryptogamic soils).

Also, a CD-ROM will be distributed with the publication featuring road and trail logs for specific parks as well as a photo glossary and gallery. The photo glossary will describe certain geologic features (i.e. what is crossbedding?). These will also be available as web-downloadable Adobe Acrobat PDF files. The UGA cannot copyright this material because it is funded with state money, so it can be distributed widely and freely, which will also benefit the purposes of the GRI. Additional reprints are not a problem because of the digital nature of the publication and the UGA board is committed to additional printings as needed. UGA normally prints 1000 copies of their publications because they become dated after about five years; that will probably not be an issue for this publication. Prices for the full-color guidebook are estimated to be approximately $25/copy, and sales are expected to be high (exact estimates for Capitol Reef NM were 125 copies/year). A website for the guidebook is forthcoming in October 1999.

Field Trips will be held in September 2000. Currently, four field trips are scheduled:
Arches NP, Canyonlands NP, Dead Horse Point State Park (SP)
Antelope Island SP and Wasatch Mountain SP
Zion NP, Cedar Breaks NM, Snow Canyon SP and Quail Creek SP
Dinosaur NM, Flaming Gorge NRA, and Red Fleet SP

Note: Trips 1 and 2 will run concurrently and Trips 3 and 4 will also run concurrently.

Many other benefits are anticipated from this publication and are enumerated below:

This type of project could serve as a model for other states to follow to bolster tourism and book sales promoting their state and its geologic features.

Sandy Eldredge (UGS) will be targeting teaching communities for involvement in the field trips; hopefully teachers will pass on what they have learned to their young audience.

The language is intended to appeal to someone with a moderate background in geology and yet will be very informative to the educated geologist. The publication may be able to serve as a textbook to colleges teaching Geology of National Parks (in Utah).

A welcomed by-product could be roadlogs between parks in Utah for those visiting multiple parks, perhaps with a regional synthesis summarizing how the overall picture of Utah geology has developed.

Paleontological Resources

Dave Sharrow is interested in having a Paleontological Survey conducted for Cedar Breaks National Monument. Similar studies have been done at Zion, Yellowstone and Death Valley. Vince Santucci (NPS-GRD Paleontologist) needs to be contacted for his input on this matter. Similar surveys have been done for Yellowstone and Death Valley NP's and have shed valuable new information on previously unrecognized resources. These surveys involve a literature review/bibliography and recognition of type specimens, species lists, and maps (which are unpublished to protect locality information), and also make park specific recommendations for protecting and preserving the resources.

The Death Valley Survey will be available soon. The Yellowstone Survey is already available on-line:

http://www.nature.nps.gov/grd/geology/paleo/yell_survey/index.htm

and is also available as a downloadable PDF at http://www.nature.nps.gov/grd/geology/paleo/yell.pdf

If a paleontological survey yields significant findings, paleontological resource management plans should be produced for Cedar Breaks involving some inventory and monitoring to identify human and natural threats to these resources. Perhaps someone on the park staff could be assigned to coordinate paleontological resource management and incorporate any findings or suggestions into the parks general management plan (GMP). It would be useful to train park staff (including interpreters and law enforcement) in resource protection, as the fossil trade "black market" has become quite lucrative for sellers and often results in illegal collecting from federal lands.

Collections taken from this area that now reside in outside repositories should be tracked down for inventory purposes. Fossils offer many interpretive themes and combine a geology/biology link and should be utilized as much as possible in interpretive programs.

Cooperative Geologic Mapping Efforts for Cedar Breaks National Monument

UGS Perspective
Currently, the UGS is mapping in Utah at three different scales: 1:24,000 for high priority areas (i.e. National and State parks), 1:100,000 for the rest of the state, and 1:500,000 for a compiled state geologic map.

The availability of funding for Cedar Breaks and Zion (jointly with the NPS) has made it possible for these higher priority areas to be mapped at this detail. The UGS plans to complete mapping for the entire state of Utah within 10-15 years at 1:100,000 scale.

For 1:100,000 scale maps, their goal is to produce both paper and digital maps; for 1:24,000 scale maps, the only digital products will be from "special interest" areas (i.e. areas such as Zion and growing metropolitan St. George). Grant Willis mentioned that the UGS simply does not have enough manpower and resources to do more areas at this scale. He also reiterated that UGS mapping goals are coincident with those of the National Geologic Mapping Program.

In Cedar Breaks NM, the UGS has been jointly cooperating with the NPS and USGS for some time on producing these 1:24,000 quadrangles in both paper and digital format. Until 1995, the USGS had done major mapping projects under the BARCO (Basin and Range to Colorado Plateau transition project) mapping program. When the USGS reorganized, many of these projects were put on indefinite hold. Fortunately, their has been mutual cooperation between the UGS and USGS to work together to get these products completed for the NPS. The NPS appreciates the labor of all involved parties and individuals in this cooperative and hopes that many products will result from the combined efforts of all involved agencies.

The UGS has divided their mapping work in the Cedar Breaks / Zion areas into two distinct phases. The first phase involves producing geologic maps for the following quadrangles (see Appendix C, Cedar Breaks NM Index of Geologic Maps, 1:24,000 Scale):
The Guardian Angels (ZION)
Temple of Sinawava (ZION)
Clear Creek Mountain (ZION)
Springdale West (ZION)
Springdale East (ZION)

All five quadrangles are field mapped and are presently in the internal review stage by the UGS; some field spot-checking is desirable. Some of the mapping was done using photogrammetric methods and some is hand drawn on Mylar. The UGS expects to deliver both completed paper and digital products by October 1, 1999.

The original projected deliverable date was April 1, 1999; however, the UGS has had significant turnover with their GIS personnel and has received an extension until October 1st 1999.

The second phase began in spring 1999 and will involve geologic mapping for the following quadrangles:
Kolob Arch (ZION)
Kolob Reservoir (ZION)
Cogswell Point (ZION)
Completion of Smith Mesa (ZION), The Barracks (ZION), and Navajo Lake (CEBR)

The Barracks (southeast of Zion NP) and Navajo Lake (south part of Cedar Breaks NM) are already available as published Open File paper maps and will be digitized as part of this phase. Deliverable dates for this phase should be September 2001 according to Grant Willis.

Some issues have surfaced regarding the correlation of Quaternary deposits across quadrangle boundaries, which has caused some delay in matching edges between maps of the USGS BARCO project and those of the UGS. The UGS would like to treat these deposits more in-depth.

USGS Perspective

Pete Rowley (USGS) talked about the immense scope of the BARCO project for preparing 1:100,000 scale maps for earthquake potential, mineral resources and various other themes. Mapping was done at 1:24,000 scale and compiled at 1:100,000 scale. Unfortunately, this project was put on the back shelf because of the USGS 1995 reorganization and many of the original workers have not been able to realize final products for their previous mapping efforts.

Since the USGS now requires digital geologic maps for all of their work, Pete is working with Southern Utah University's (SUU) Dave Maxwell to complete digitizing for some of the BARCO work.

There are many 7.5-minute quadrangles in the BRCA, ZION, and CEBR areas that are in various stages of completion from USGS personnel; Pete Rowley hopes that he will be able to help tidy up some of these unfinished maps and make them ready for publication.

As the park's hydrologist, Dave Sharrow would like to see some emphasis on studying the quadrangles east of Zion for water issues. These include the Webster Flat and Orderville quadrangles. From his perspective those closest to the Sevier fault are of most interest to him because of a lack of understanding of the hydrology nearest the fault. Pete has done a similar type of project for Nevada test site and would be willing to further discuss this with Dave Sharrow.

Current Status
Two 7.5-minute quadrangles cover Cedar Breaks NM: Brians Head to the north, and Navajo Lake to the south. Flanigan Arch is to the immediate west of Brians Head, and Webster Flat is west of Navajo Lake; both are not on NPS land. (see figure 11, Cedar Breaks NM Index of Geologic Maps, 1:24,000 Scale):

Navajo Lake is published by the USGS as OF (Open File) Report 93-190 entitled "Preliminary Geologic Map of Navajo Lake Quadrangle, Kane and Iron Counties, Utah" by David Moore and David Nealey, and was published in 1993. Grant Willis thought that the Quaternary could use some updating, however. Once agreement on the quality of the Quaternary is reached, this quadrangle could be digitized at SUU under the supervision of Pete Rowley.

Existing funding is available to digitize this quadrangle under the current agreement between the NPS and UGS for Zion and Cedar Breaks. Grant Willis needs to make sure that digitization at SUU can be contracted through the UGS; he will report back on this. All present thought that this was a good idea, as Pete Rowley would be able to supervise the work out of SUU, and it would serve as a good exercise for SUU, should they receive more of the BARCO quadrangles for digitization.

Brians Head and Flanigan Arch are very near completion as Pete Rowley held up drafts of the two quadrangles that Ed Sable had been working on. Ed's deteriorating health, coupled with the collapse of the BARCO project did not allow him to complete these quadrangles. Pete is willing to take over these projects and complete deliverables if funding can be secured. The NPS may be able to secure funding to complete the Brians Head quadrangle, since it does fall within the Cedar Breaks boundary.

It was requested of Tom Henry (CEBR superintendent) and Don Falvey (ZION superintendent) that they request the services of Pete Rowley from the USGS to complete the geologic mapping; GRD can assist with writing such a request if they so desire. Pete suggests that Sable remain the senior author and Rowley and Hatfield as co-authors. Rowley would prepare cross-sections, text and do all field checking.

Other Miscellaneous loose ends: Pete prepared a list of other regional quadrangles and categorized them as to the status of field mapping and producing paper maps as "mostly done", "work still needed", and "USGS published quads", as follows:

Mostly done	Work Still Needed	USGS Published Quadrangles
Flanigan Arch Brian Head Red Creek Reservoir Five Mile Ridge Summit	Kolob Reservoir Cogswell Point Straight Canyon Haycock Mountain Panguitch Lake Henrie Knolls	Navajo Lake Cedar City Kannarraville Cedar Mountain Parowan Paragonah Parowan Gap Cottonwood Mountain Little Creek Peak Hatch Asay Bench

Flanigan Arch and Webster Flat are of interest to CEBR and ZION because of the regional watershed, and may be able to be treated as "quadrangles of interest" to the NPS. Again, much preliminary fieldwork has been on these quadrangles by the USGS BARCO team.

Pete Rowley also mentioned that the USGS has agreed to fund the digitization of the Kanab 1:100,000 quadrangle through SUU, and hopes to begin overseeing this project in the very near future. Kanab greenlines are also available. The Panguitch 100,000 quadrangle has also been digitized by Florian Maldonado (USGS- Denver) in his spare time.

There are some issues to consider in completing these quadrangles:
Pete would need some financial assistance in digitizing these maps at SUU. Dave Maxwell is willing and able to get a GIS shop going on BARCO projects as he has sufficient equipment and personnel. With Pete's oversight and input, it is hoped that many products may result from the SUU GIS department. Dave Maxwell would also like to get with the UGS for his input on how to scope out these digital geology projects.

An EDMAP project may be a good way to obtain assistance for completing any needed field mapping with SUU students

Pete's salary and time needs to be covered by the USGS to work on this project. Bruce Heise (NPS- GRD) requested a proposal for Pete Rowley's time to complete the quadrangles of interest to CEBR and ZION that were started under the BARCO project and need some work to produce final products.

It may be possible to tap into the National Mapping program to obtain financial assistance here. A two-tier proposal was suggested: first just to complete Brian Head, and second to include the western quadrangles (Flanigan Arch and Webster Flat) with Brian Head.

Other surficial specialists (Van Williams was mentioned) may need to be called upon to help complete the surficial mapping and caliche deposits; also numerous landslides are known for the area and should be mapped appropriately. Salary and time is also an issue for these specialists.

A priority list for quadrangles of interest should be developed for SUU and estimates of costs and time to complete the work also need to be ascertained. Grant Willis suggested that a few weeks for a single quadrangle seems like a reasonable amount of time.

Other Sources of Natural Resources Data for Cedar Breaks
The UGS has a significant quadrangle database that they have furnished to NRID for the entire state of Utah.

NRID has compiled a geologic bibliography for numerous parks and monuments, including Cedar Breaks. Visit the website: http://165.83.36.151/biblios/geobib.nsf; user id is "geobib read", password is "anybody".

The USGS has compiled large volumes of data on the BARCO project that was halted in 1995; much of this work is unpublished and should be sought out from USGS personnel.

Dave Sharrow was asked if CEBR currently has their ProCite software in place that chronicle any natural resources into a bibliography. Dave was not sure, and thought that Steve Robinson would know for sure. Steve needs consulted on this.

Pete Rowley circulated a few articles by John Anderson that are available as UGS publications, and are also contained in the geologic bibliography for CEBR.

Dave Sharrow mentioned that a new water well will be drilled on a fault trace near the visitor center observation platform; well logs generated from this activity will be of interest to GRD, WRD and CEBR.

Geologic Hazards

The main geologic hazard discussed for CEBR centers around overlooks and fractures within the Claron Formation and how safe they are. It was agreed that all overlooks should be monitored for fracturing. Tom Henry would like some assurances from geologists about the stability of the overlooks. Siting facilities is also a major issue because of the fractures and potential for sloughing; these areas should be monitored for growth and potential danger.

Potential Research Topics Cedar Breaks National Monument

It was mentioned by Tom Henry that the Thomas Bill is emphasizing research by local cooperators that provides information to management and is applicable to interpretation of resources. Integration of this with SUU should be taken advantage of. For a quick review of the Thomas Bill go to the following website:

http://rs9.loc.gov/cgi-bin/bdquery/z?d105:SN01693:|TOM:/bss/d105query.html

A list of potential research topics includes studies of the following:

- A detailed study of the Claron Formation
- Study chert distribution around CEBR as it has numerous cultural implications as well
- Develop the fire history from bogs for the last 20,000 years; Lowder Creek goes back 17,000; Red Valley 11,000; 3000 for Alpine Pond.
- Study of the groundwater system; there is lots of precipitation and little coming out of the rocks; where is it going? CEBR is especially concerned about a drinking water supply and enough to flush toilets
- In relation to the groundwater is a relatively unexplored cave and karst system that could use additional investigation; surface sinkholes suggest a well-developed system that should be studied; consult with Ron Kerbo (NPS- GRD Cave Specialist)
- Look at surface water in relation to forest canopy; decreased canopy should increase evapotranspiration
- Look at discharge rates of surface water
- Glacial/megabreccia needs investigation around Brian Head peak; nothing published by the people Grant mentioned (Gary Player)

- Isom Formation Study
- Study clustered vegetation and relation to the bedrock strata; geologic controls on locations of vegetation
- Study of rates of erosion and fractures along visitor overlooks
- Any CEBR/BRCA joint research possibilities should be lumped (Claron, erosion rates)
- Catalog unique geologic features; obtain GIS data for unique geologic features of CEBR; Dave Maxwell has students that are required to do research and he can offer their assistance like they are doing at BRCA. SUU may become a center of GIS excellence in association with Trimble Navigation
- Consult with John Anderson on any ideas he may have for research
- Attempt to better understand the dune/mud deposits on the rim shown by Laird Naylor during the field trip; geology and archeology interact here
- Better understand the role of CEBR in the transition between the Basin and Range and Colorado Plateau physiographic provinces; develop interpretive display at CEBR or Brian Head for this

Action Items

Many follow-up items were discussed during the course of the scoping session and are reiterated by category for quick reference.

Interpretation

More graphics and brochures emphasizing the transition between the Basin and Range and Colorado Plateau targeting the average enthusiast should be developed. If Cedar Breaks NP needs assistance with these, please consult GRD's Jim Wood (jim_f_wood@nps.gov) or Melanie Moreno at the USGS- Menlo Park, CA (mmoreno@usgs.gov).

UGA Guidebook

Attempt to plant the seeds of this concept to other states for similar publications involving local area geology. Such publications are especially useful for the GRI

Paleontological Resources

Consult with Vince Santucci on the likelihood of a full paleontological survey for CEBR

Geologic Mapping

Maintain UGS- USGS- NPS cooperation to reap all possible products from existing USGS BARCO work to benefit the NPS GRI

USGS address issues relating to funding salaries and other work to ensure BARCO products can be published

USGS develop for SUU a priority list of quadrangles to digitize and complete field mapping, as well as associated estimates of time and material costs

Pete Rowley prepare a 2- tier cost proposal for his services to complete geologic field mapping of area quadrangles

Attempt to obtain letters from the CEBR and ZION superintendents requesting the services of the USGS to complete geologic mapping of quadrangles of interest for this region. The UGS has requested similar favors of the USGS in the Marysvale area.

Grant Willis needs to make sure that the Navajo Lake quadrangle can be transferred to SUU for digitizing since it is part of an existing agreement.

Natural Resource Data Sources

Consult with Steve Robinson to see if ProCite database is in place for CEBR

Miscellaneous

Dave Sharrow would like to receive a "contact list" for UGS staff from Grant Willis
Review proposed research topics for future studies within Cedar Breaks NP
Make contact with USGS GIS person Jeremy Workman to develop relationship with NPS GIS projects
Have conference call with Gregson, Heise, Connors and Maxwell to discuss potential future projects, including possible digitization of the BRCA maps by Bill Bowers (1990)

Scoping Meeting Attendees

Name	Affiliation	Phone	e- mail
Bruce Heise	NPS, Geologic Resources Division	(303) 969- 2017	Bruce_Hiese@nps.gov
Stephanie O'Meara	CSU, Research Associate	(970) 225- 3567	Stephanie_O'Meara@partner.nps.gov
Tim Connors	NPS, Geologic Resources Division	(303) 969- 2093	Tim_Connors@nps.gov
Pete Rowley	USGS	(435) 865- 5928	prowley@usgs.gov
Grant Willis	Utah Geological Survey	(801) 537- 3355	Nrugs.gwillis@state.ut.us
Dave Maxwell	SUU, GIS	(435) 865- 8313	maxwell@suu.edu
Dave Sharrow	NPS- CEBR, Hydrologist	(435) 586- 9451	Dave_Sharrow@nps.gov
Steve Robinson	NPS- CEBR, Ranger	(435) 586- 9451	Steve_Robinson@nps.gov
Tom Henry	NPS- CEBR, Superintendent	(435) 586- 9451	Tom_Henry@nps.gov
Stan Hatfield	SUU, Geology Dept.	(435) 865- 8160	hatfield@suu.edu
Laird Naylor	UT BLM; formerly CEBR Archeologist	(801) 977- 4357	lnaylor@ut.blm.gov
Danielle Rousseau	NPS, Geologic Resources Division	(303) 987- 6925	Danielle_Rousseau@nps.gov
Michael Hozik	Richard Stockton College of NJ	(609) 652- 4277	Hozikm@loki.stockton.edu
Christy Stauffer	USDA FS	(435) 865- 3242	Cistauffer@netutah.com
Bill Case	UGS, Extension Services	(801) 537- 3340	Nrug.bcase@state.ut.us

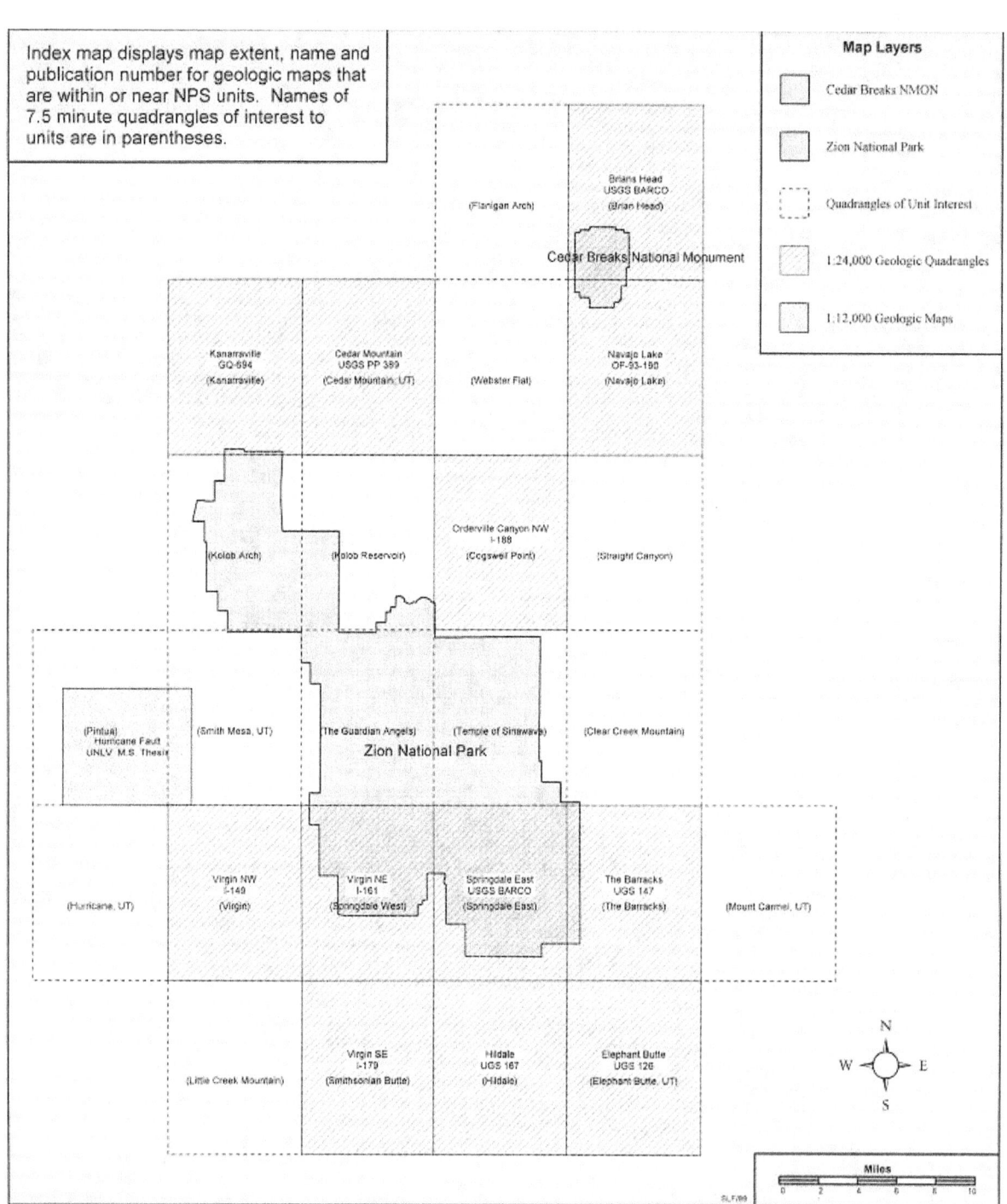

Index map displays map extent, name and publication number for geologic maps that are within or near NPS units. Names of 7.5 minute quadrangles of interest to units are in parentheses.

Map Layers

- Cedar Breaks NMON
- Zion National Park
- Quadrangles of Unit Interest
- 1:24,000 Geologic Quadrangles
- 1:12,000 Geologic Maps

Brians Head
USGS BARCO
(Brian Head)

(Flanigan Arch)

Cedar Breaks National Monument

Kanarraville
GQ-694
(Kanarraville)

Cedar Mountain
USGS PP 389
(Cedar Mountain, UT)

(Webster Flat)

Navajo Lake
OF-93-180
(Navajo Lake)

Orderville Canyon NW
I-188
(Cogswell Point)

(Kolob Arch)

(Kolob Reservoir)

(Straight Canyon)

(Pintura)
Hurricane Fault
UNLV M.S. Thesis

(Smith Mesa, UT)

The Guardian Angels

(Temple of Sinawava)

(Clear Creek Mountain)

Zion National Park

Virgin NW
I-149

Virgin NE
I-161

Springdale East
USGS 147

The Barracks
UGS 147

(Hurricane, UT)

(Virgin)

(Springdale West)

Springdale East
USGS BARCO
(Springdale East)

(The Barracks)

(Mount Carmel, UT)

Virgin SE
I-179

Hildale
UGS 167

Elephant Butte
UGS 128

(Little Creek Mountain)

(Smithsonian Butte)

(Hildale)

(Elephant Butte, UT)

N
W — E
S

Miles
0   2   4   6   8   10

Map coverage of Cedar Breaks National Monument at the scale of 1:24,000. From GRE Scoping Report

Cedar Breaks National Monument
Geologic Resource Evaluation Report

Natural Resource Report NPS/NRPC/GRD/NRR—2006/006
NPS D-215, March 2006

National Park Service
Director • Fran P. Mainella

Natural Resource Stewardship and Science
Associate Director • Michael A. Soukup

Natural Resource Program Center
The Natural Resource Program Center (NRPC) is the core of the NPS Natural Resource Stewardship and Science Directorate. The Center Director is located in Fort Collins, with staff located principally in Lakewood and Fort Collins, Colorado and in Washington, D.C. The NRPC has five divisions: Air Resources Division, Biological Resource Management Division, Environmental Quality Division, Geologic Resources Division, and Water Resources Division. NRPC also includes three offices: The Office of Education and Outreach, the Office of Inventory, Monitoring and Evaluation, and the Office of Natural Resource Information Systems. In addition, Natural Resource Web Management and Partnership Coordination are cross-cutting disciplines under the Center Director. The multidisciplinary staff of NRPC is dedicated to resolving park resource management challenges originating in and outside units of the national park system.

Geologic Resources Division
Chief • David B. Shaver
Planning Evaluation and Permits Branch Chief • Carol McCoy

Credits
Author • Trista Thornberry-Ehrlich
Editing • Sid Covington
Digital Map Production • Victor DeWolfe, Stephanie O'Meara, and Dave Maxwell
Map Layout Design • Melanie Ransmeier